CANNES ENCORE!

TRAVEL IN THE TIME OF COVID

LES STANLEY
TRACY STANLEY

Copyright © Les Stanley Tracy Stanley 2022

The moral right of the author has been asserted.

All rights reserved. No part of this publication may be reproduced, or transmitted by any person or entity (including Google, Amazon or similar organisations), in any form or by any means electronic or mechanical, including photocopying, recording, scanning or by any information storage and retrieval system or transmitted in any form, or by any means without the prior written permission without prior permission in writing from the publisher.

A catalogue record for this book is available from the National Library of Australia.

Ebook – Kindle
978-0-6451358-5-5

Paperback
978-0-6451358-6-2

Cover Design by nabinkarna on Fiverr

www.lesstanley.com
www.tjstanley.com

L'enfer, c'est les autres. Hell is other people.
Front cover quote taken from Jean-Paul Sartre's play - No Exit

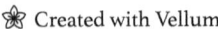 Created with Vellum

CONTENTS

Foreword from Jeff Stoward	1
Advance Praise for Cannes Encore	4

PRE-DEPARTURE

Tracy – Waiting for take-off	9
Les – My travel goals	13

PART I
LEAVING BRISBANE

Tracy – Ticking things off	17
Les – At the airport	18
Tracy – The inflight experience	21
Les – On the plane	23

PART II
VIVE LA FRANCE

Les – Jet lag	29
Tracy – Longing for sleep	31
Les – Sensitive neighbours	33
Tracy – Le Bank	35
Les – Waiting for cappuccini	36
Tracy – French bureaucracy	39
Les – The other Cannes	41
Tracy – Sojourn to Sophia Antipolis	43
Les – Day trip to Italy	45
Tracy – Unwelcome message	47
Tracy – Moans in the morning.	49
Les – Andiamo	50
Tracy – Theoule sur Mer	54
Tracy – Back to the bank in Cannes	58
Tracy – Old Antibes	60
Les – To bank or not to bank	63
Tracy – Oh Joy Oh Joy	66

Les – A surprising bureaucratic success	68
Tracy – Day trip to Nice	71
Les - A lucky escape	77
Les – Once more, down to the beach	79
Tracy – Ile Sainte Marguerite	80
Tracy – Departing for Paris by TGV	83
Les – Searching for Henry Miller	91
Tracy – Visiting Victor Hugo's house	96
Tracy – At Gare du Nord - Off to London	99

PART III

THE UNITED KINGDOM IN THE TIME OF BORIS

Tracy – Sunny day in Sutton	103
Les – Just one Beatle	104
Tracy –Train strikes	106
Tracy – Visiting the Scottish Parliament	109
Les – Another day indoors in Edinburgh	112
Les – Heading South	114
Tracy – Back in Sutton	116
Les – Meeting famous people in Sutton	122
Les – Catching up with old friends	125
Tracy - Day 6 of COVID	127
Les – Independence Day	130
Tracy - Tot ziens	133
Les - Looking for a charger	140

PART IV

CHUGGING THROUGH THE CONTINENT

German Beer, Thai Food	145
The German for Mosquito	149
An early bath and a late train	151
Toilet budgets	153
A Day trip to Lübeck.	156
Without the Beatles	158
Visiting Lüneburg	160
Trying again	163
Technology challenges	166

Which way?	169
Herne Bay of the North	171
Hot, hotter, hottest	173
Escaping the heat	175
Copenhagen memories	180
Other Songs	184
More of Denmark	187

PART V
BACK TO THE KINGDOM OF THAILAND

Train to the airport	193
Arrival in Bangkok	197
Counting my teeth	201
A visit to the hospital	203
Hidden Holiday House	207

PART VI
COMING HOME

Homeward bound	211
Back home	215
A few words from the authors	220
About Les Stanley	221
About Tracy Stanley	223
Soft Nut Bike Tour of Burma	225
My Brother's Bicycle	227
Our social media hangouts	229

FOREWORD FROM JEFF STOWARD

I've always had a love of travel, especially European travel, so when Les and Tracy told me they were off to the U.K. and other places smart enough to remain committed to a common market, I was envious. No, that's not entirely true – I was jealous.

As an author myself who writes about Europe, I wanted it to be me. But some of us have jobs and commitments and can't ponce around Europe quaffing cappuccinos and complaining about the service ethos of French waiters for a living. So, I was somewhat mollified when they asked me to provide a foreword for their very funny tale of two Europes – Tracy's, which was all about catching up with friends (and catching Covid); and the version that Les provides, which focussed more on plaques and catching the 21st century equivalent of the plague as well. But we'll get to that in due course.

As a grumpy old man myself, I 'get' Les. I'd like to add some of his other qualities, like his cynicism and impatience, but since he asked me to write this forward, I won't. He does, however, enjoy searching for obscure and unusual historical monuments, so there's that I suppose. And as a likeminded 'free spirit' who would love nothing better than to hop on a plane with an overnight bag, we'd be good travel partners, at least in theory.

But, like Les, I need my partner, Monica, to ensure my dreams become a reality – not a nightmare – so that's why his 'child bride' Tracy is the perfect accompaniment. Throughout this tale of two trips, she tries to keep him in line, much like my wife does, keeping his crankiness in check until they part ways later in the story.

But as I read 'Cannes Encore!' I came to the realisation that travelling with Les would have had its 'challenges'. I bet he likes to drink warm lager and I know he doesn't care for sports, so we'd have little in common. Except for travel, writing about travel, doing as little work as possible and blaming the French for anything and everything. Kindred spirits actually.

I particularly liked his take on the youth of society and where they have gone wrong – feckless youth be damned. But that just might be a symptom of our advanced years. I couldn't help but be reminded of Dylan Thomas, who wrote –

"Do not go gentle into that good night.
 Rage, rage against the dying of the light".

After paying too much for bitter dishwater across the south of France, Les and Tracy head to Covid Central (sorry, Britain) for their unique take on what constitutes a good English breakfast, before they take flight in different directions – Tracy back home to Australia and Les on a pilgrimage to revisit his youth, back on 'the continent' and then, via Thailand, home.

I found it hard to put down, but that was probably because it was more fun reading this book than doing my day job.

Anyway, I can't recommend 'Cannes Encore' enough – if you dream of experiencing Europe, all whilst taking in some lessons learned on what NOT to do, this is your book. Especially if you struggle with pesky things like the Internet, train timetables, public conveniences, and people in general. I can't wait to apply what I've learnt on my next "European Nonsense" adventure! (that may or may not be a plug for another book).

Jeff Stoward, Author of European Nonsense
www.jeffstoward.com

ADVANCE PRAISE FOR CANNES ENCORE

This book was an amusing read. Until I reflected a bit and realised that it was quite a sad story about a nobody searching for meaning, symptomatic of the nobodies I had surrounded myself with in my life. This probably meant I was a nobody too. This then depressed my mood. There were shades of James Thurber & Franz Kafka in the style. This may be a good thing, I'm not sure.

Chris Adams - French tutor and occasional friend

Most of what follows actually happened.

PRE-DEPARTURE

Never been happier

TRACY – WAITING FOR TAKE-OFF

The pandemic was frustrating for my husband, Les, as it surely was for many other people. He'd officially retired a few months previously and his, somewhat vague, plan was to *travel and write*. When asked, "won't you be bored now you're not working?" his favourite response was, "maybe, but I was pretty bored at work most of the time." Working was the last thing he wanted to do.

Then COVID came along. So, unable to go anywhere, he returned to work to occupy the time he should have been travelling. The enforced landlubber status was destroying his adventurous ambitions for his retirement. He was all too aware of steadily approaching ailments such as a bothersome back and a kinking knee – all reminding him of his advancing age. The clock was ticking loudly in his head.

. . .

My husband is not a fan of other people. He's sliding, less than gracefully, into his natural persona of grumpy old man. He's adamant that it's not him who's grumpy, it's other people who are irritating, dithering or too noisy. The irony is that my husband imagines himself as a free spirit. Open. Tolerant. Worldly.

A change of habits

There is a challenge in travelling with others; husband, boyfriend, girlfriend, anyone really. After thirty plus years of marriage, you would have thought that I'd be used to the close and personal contact required for traipsing across the continent... But no. Travel requires intimate, often 24-hour close proximity. It can be an intense experience when you're removed from the comfort of your daily habits and customs, you're confronted by multiple decisions on how to travel, e.g., walk, bus, taxi and where to stop, eat and drink. And then we have the challenge of choosing accommodation. Self-outing here that I like to have my accommodation booked in advance, whereas Les, when it's practical, likes to rock into town and choose somewhere that meets his criteria for charming, quiet, inexpensive, with delightful hosts and not too far from the railway station. This idea is lovely but the stress of not finding this little nugget, both pre-anticipated and experienced first-hand on arrival, removes the joy of travelling for me. It's just too easy to arrive to discover that a local literary, food tasting or cycling festival has meant that the only accommodation available is 13 miles out of town and not accessible by public transport.

Just bring hand luggage…

But let me not get too far ahead of myself. I need to mention Les' fantasy of travelling for several months across countries of varying temperatures – with only hand luggage. Yes, this is something you can do, if your spouse has checked in luggage that includes, shampoo, Gaviscon tablets, mosquito repellent, an extra t-shirt and pair of socks, first aid kit, spare battery charger, you get the idea.

Curiously, one thing that he always packs, which I think is completely unnecessary, are peanut butter sandwiches. Did I mention that my spouse likes to pack light, taking only the barest of essentials? But still, there's room for sandwiches which is absurd given that the trolley passes every three hours, and that snacks can be obtained through the gentle push of a button. He reminds me, that on many flights, food is served at ridiculous times, "Chicken or beef at 2.30 in the morning, sir?" Also, that, with more and more low-cost carriers not providing food at all having a couple of surreptitious sandwiches tucked away can save money. I know that economy-class airline food is not gourmet, but it more than meets basic sustenance requirements. And sitting for hours on end as we cross ocean after ocean and an occasional land mass, does not burn calories.

I need alone-time

Self-declaration. I love being on my own; I need time alone – and travelling together makes this nearly impossible. We are in each other's company 24 hours a day. I think I must be an introvert although this would surprise many. I'd rather be in the outback with kookaburras for company than queuing with dozens of others in need of a steaming cappuccino – and I love cappuccinos. It's hard work being an explorer and with all those decisions and other people, indeed a stressful experience.

LES – MY TRAVEL GOALS

I made several plans for this, my first trip overseas since the onslaught of COVID.

Travelwise these mainly comprised extensive train journeys through Turkey and Europe along with lengthy stays in Italy, France, The UK, Germany and Scandinavia.

On the nostalgia front, surely an important part of travel as age takes its toll, I wanted to revisit places already seen. Preferably those with happy memories.

I was also keen to keep up my age-deflecting health regime of maintaining an average of 10,000 steps a day.

Plus of course, I was keen not to catch COVID.

This is what happened.

PART I
LEAVING BRISBANE

TRACY – TICKING THINGS OFF

We are slowly ticking off the things to do before we go away. It's a good feeling. Most important is the COVID insurance. My cousin has recently caught COVID on the last day of his European travel tour. He reported he was quickly burning thru his travel insurance because he was in Monaco during a special event – so accommodation was expensive (even more than usual) and he needed to get his food delivered to his hotel room.

I created the #EurAsia22 hashtag and began a hopeful, and ultimately unsuccessful twitter campaign to let Emirates know we were travel writers who were soon to board a flight to Nice via Dubai. Perhaps they might upgrade us so that we could partake of the bar in the sky? I know this is every economy traveller's fantasy. An unexpected gift. An opportunity to move up class and comfort level.

LES – AT THE AIRPORT

After an uneventful taxi ride through the early evening Brisbane streets, we arrived, far too early, at the airport. Check in had just opened and we dutifully took our place in the appropriate queue, clutching various documents. Thirty minutes later, a friendly check in agent informed us that, as our final destination was the city of Nice, we needed to complete something called a *Sworn*. This turned out to be an item specifically for entry into bureaucracy loving France. We filled out the form stating, among other things, that neither of us had been suffering from *headaches or any other unusual symptoms* recently.

As we passed through security, I made my first mistake of the trip by discarding my recently empty water bottle instead of keeping it to refill later. This necessitated me spending the extortionate sum of $4.50 to replace it. My only excuse for this schoolboy error was that, having been reminded numerous times by both recorded messages and colourful posters, emblazoned throughout the otherwise drab, airport building, that *masks must be worn*, I was asked to remove my mask when I passed through passport control. This had increase my paranoia and I mistakenly assumed that water bottles also needed to be discarded at all times.

Fear of COVID had replaced fear of a terrorist boarding a plane with a plastic bottle full of petrol. I remembered that once when travelling in India, the security check had involved making people take a sip from the bottle to prove it contained nothing dangerous. I thought this odd as surely, anyone deluded or desperate enough to want to blow up a plane and hundreds of innocent people, along with themselves, would not think twice about swallowing a bit of petrol.

In the departures lounge, we looked around for somewhere quiet and comfortable to sit. Our first requirement was easy to obtain as the hall was almost empty. Finding anywhere even reasonably comfortable was a challenge though, as the airport authorities seemed to have made the decision to buy their seating from the Broadbangian branch of IKEA and every chair was almost twice as big as it needed to be. This had the effect of making any attempt to sit in it, result immediately in sliding down into a slumped position, not conducive to relaxation, or indeed good for any level of lumbar support. It was pretty obvious to me that this apparent design fault was actually a cunning ploy by the only restaurant that was open to attract customers, as it had a wide variety of comfy looking chairs tantalisingly within reach. Back problems being one of the many ailments I had started to endure, I was keen not to exacerbate the issue so early in the trip. After thirty minutes or so of shifting around in the oversize wooden chairs in the departure's hall, I went to investigate other options at our gate. Fortunately, there was much more choice there and we relocated to wait in relative comfort for the two hours before our plane departed.

Time passed slowly but eventually we were called for boarding. On board we took our seats and waited again for the plane to fill. So much of travel consists of waiting for something. Eventually, after thirty minutes or so of taxiing, where we went from one end of the runway to the other and back again, I guess the wind changed, the captain powered up the engines and we took off into the Brisbane night. Only fourteen and a half hours to go.

TRACY – THE INFLIGHT EXPERIENCE

Our flight was packed and delightfully all passengers were mask-wearing-compliant. Very impressed with Emirates and the steps they were taking to keep everyone healthy, including regular reminders on our screen to keep our masks on and a prompt for us to remind others to do the same. There was widespread compliance until we arrived in Nice many hours later, and all the 'Frenchies' removed theirs.

We were initially, slightly concerned by the high number of young children boarding. Eventually, we realised that we were witnessing one of the effects of the easing of travel restrictions. The hordes of toddlers were obviously born during the COVID period and were now on their first flight to visit their grandparents. While they were boisterous in the airport, once on board, they were thankfully quiet and, for the most part, slept. Comfortably settled, I alternated between being mesmerised by the flight journey animation screen and listening to the

Emirates radio station. They were both excellent and it crossed my mind that next time we should stop in Dubai so we can visit a rainforest in the desert, experience a Museum of the Future and perhaps go swimming with piranhas–while they are feeding! This idea, must have resulted from a particularly bizarre team meeting.

LES – ON THE PLANE

I watched a couple of movies I'd seen before, a few episodes of a TV series I like and my wife hates, (Larry David's Curb Your Enthusiasm), listened to some music and audio books, dozed and ate whatever was offered. Slowly, the time passed. I awoke from my fourth or fifth nap thinking, surely, we must be nearly there by now. But no, I was dismayed to see, from the detailed map provided, we had just crossed the coastline of Eastern India and still had around five hours to go before landing in Dubai. And this was just the first leg of the journey. I dozed some more. I became so desperate, I even engaged the passenger seated next to me in idle conversation. Eventually we began our descent into the early morning sunlight of Dubai.

Our connecting flight left from the same terminal, Dubai has three, and I had naively assumed we would be able to simply walk to the new departure gate. No such luck. We were herded onto a bus, which did not depart until it was uncomfortably overcrowded. It then proceeded to drive, and drive, and drive towards our departure gate. One highlight of this, journey within a journey, was that at one stage we were driving parallel to a taxiway and our small overcrowded bus was travelling at the same speed as a taxiing aircraft. The race continued for several seconds but was too soon over as the plane veered off to majestically take to the sky. Presumably to head off to some exotic destination, while our bus continued its trundling progress.

We eventually arrived at the gate and obediently shuffled inside to wait for our connecting flight. To pass the time while we waited, and unaware of the exchange rate, I bought, what turned out to be, one of the most expensive coffees of my life at Starbucks. As I was to discover when we arrived in France, this struggle with all things caffeine related was to continue.

Les – On the plane

Smiling EK Ladies

PART II

VIVE LA FRANCE

LES – JET LAG

Our arrival in Cannes, France coincided with the final day of the film festival and much disassembling of stages, camera equipment and other paraphernalia was going on. We walked the streets for a while, a couple of wide-eyed tourists and were soon in need of coffee, so sought out a café or boulangerie.

Keen to practise my French, I offered to order. I entered just behind someone who, judging by the number of baked items he was buying, was obviously stocking up for some kind of siege. Finally, arms fully laden with sugary treats, he departed. He was followed in line by a young woman who, I was sure, had a long-term plan to order a beverage of some kind. But, before she could place her order, she needed to carry out a lengthy interrogation regarding, not just the fruit on which various juices were based, but any other contents as well. After a while she departed, clutching a green and unappetising looking beverage, and my time finally came to order two cappuccinos.

As I brought these to the table where my wife was sitting, I was asked where the croissant was, that she had apparently requested. I re-entered the shop and stood in line again as more siege participants gave their orders to the friendly but distracted lady behind the counter. Not only was she dispensing bread and other items at an alarming rate, but seemed to be, simultaneously, conducting a second business on her mobile phone. Some minutes later, I reached the counter for the second time and ordered the all-important croissant. I returned with this, presented it to my wife and sat down to enjoy my coffee. But this was France and the coffee was bitter as well as cold. I drank it anyway.

TRACY – LONGING FOR SLEEP

Walked around Cannes today in a mental fog. Not too tired of course, to notice that we were in the minority wearing masks. I know that the heat made it even less desirable to have a swather of fabric, hammocked across your face. But COVID was still racing around the world with gay abandon. Collapsed into bed at 4:45 pm and of course woke up ready to start the new day just after midnight. Slid quietly out of bed, or so I thought, and poured myself a bowl of cereal. Returned to bed and lay awake until 5:00am. Perhaps not strangely, I'm feeling weary now as an inconsiderate bird, maniacally screeches from the roof of the house next door.

First stop of the day was a visit to the bustling Forville Marché. It is a delight for the senses with bubbling cauldrons of Provençal chicken, wide selections of fromage and rows of magnificent and heavily scented roses with a kaleidoscope of colours. There are also pastries, pasta and delicious delicatessen type fare. The market stall owners, *les vendeurs*, are part thespian, efficiently exchanging goods for money with a theatrical twinkle.

Disappointed that our favourite Italian café of Da Laura, doesn't open on a Sunday and may not be open tomorrow. Still, we take comfort in the beautiful walk along the croisette and watch the pricey water craft bobbing gently against their moorings.

LES – SENSITIVE NEIGHBOURS

Another day battling the scourge of jetlag. The previous night we'd stumbled into bed around 7pm, both having fallen asleep in front of the TV a good hour before. Sliding between the sheets in the bright-as-day sunshine, we both fell asleep immediately only to be wide awake again around 2am. The display on my phone told me that this was 10am Brisbane time, so this was perfectly logical, actually a bit of a lie-in. Unable to go back to sleep, I read and watched some light entertainment on my tablet before finally dozing off again around 4.30 for another hour or so.

We finally gave up on sleep around 6am and started our day's activities. Our plan for the day was to revisit Mandelieu, a small town nearby, where we used to live. We boarded the bus, which took us the few kilometres along the coast. Mandelieu hadn't changed much. There were a few new buildings and a couple of cafés that hadn't been there before, but it was still an undiscovered gem, albeit not a perfect one. Our old apartment was still standing and we wondered how the people who had bought it from us were faring. It's always odd going back to a previous home which holds happy memories such as convivial conversations in the stairwell and sausages sizzling on a homemade drum BBQ for the local, council promoted, *fête des voisins* or neighbours' day event each year. We took a leisurely stroll alongside the Siagne river, which runs through Mandelieu, before making our way back to Cannes.

As we arrived back at our apartment, we were met by our neighbours, who seemed to have been waiting for us. They complained bitterly about all the noise we had made early in the morning. It was hard to understand how we had disturbed them, as they were two floors below us. After listening to their tirade for a few minutes and then apologising profusely, we went on our way. Later that day, with the aid of Google, I wrote a note, in French, apologising for disturbing their slumbers and promising we would be quiet in the future. A day or so later, we bumped into them again, enjoying coffee and a cigarette on the steps near the apartment, and they were very friendly. The French love a bit of *fausse humilité*.

TRACY – LE BANK

We had made a prior arrangement to visit our bank. Les' bank card was due for renewal and we thought we might pick it up here while we were here. The Cannes branch of BNP Paribas is dedicated to their international customers, who have specific needs, or so we were told by our account manager. Our need was to have Les' pension automatically transferred to our Australian bank account on a monthly basis. *Ce n'est pas possible* we were informed. Oh well. *So can we arrange collection of Les' bank card while we are in Cannes*? Of course, and have you considered a biometric card? These new cards had a thumb print embedded. This was, I thought, an excellent technology which would mean that if someone stole our card, they couldn't use it unless they knew the PIN, or cut off our thumb. Les was less impressed, particularly with the higher annual cost, but he relented, given my arguments for the value of increased security. Just a few days and our new cards would arrive. Or so we thought.

LES – WAITING FOR CAPPUCCINI

After our successful (little did we know) visit to the bank, we deserved a real Italian cappuccino. We visited a café we had discovered many years previously. Getting a good coffee in the south of France is not an easy challenge. Of course, the situation is subjective, literally, a matter of taste, but unless you are a fan of bitter coffee, preferring, as we both do, the silky texture and flavour of the cappuccino, France is not your friend. When we lived in the area, we used to ride our bikes the few kilometres from Mandelieu to Cannes to have breakfast at Da Laura. Not before 8am though, as no self-respecting French person could possibly want breakfast so early, and certainly no-one could possibly be expected to work at that time of the day. This was an Italian owned establishment and they seemed to understand that a cappuccino is not just a coffee with some froth on the top. It was a sunny day, but we took a seat inside to avoid the wafts of smoke emanating from those seated outside, ordered and waited expectantly.

. . .

A few minutes later, we spotted a couple of cappuccini, which we assumed were ours, placed on a tray near the bar. The waiter ignored them for a while, then looked as if he was planning his route to cover the metre or so required to collect them and bring them to our table. But, at the last minute, he wavered and decided he should first take an order from a couple who had just entered. The cappuccini sat tantalisingly close, a thin veil of steam rising from the recently heated milk. The waiter returned to the vicinity of the bar but seemed not to notice the beverages and ventured outside to see if any recently arrived customers required servicing. The young lady who had made the cappuccinos moved the few feet from her steaming machine, passing within inches of the now slightly less-steaming drinks and busied herself with a small bowl of fruit which seemed to suddenly require rearranging. The waiter had by now adopted a nonchalant stance in the doorway, enjoying the view of the bustling street. Realising that the staff had no intention of doing so, I got up and took the drinks to our table myself, vowing to leave no tip or indeed ever to return.

The following day, in our ongoing quest for a drinkable cappuccino, we ventured into a café we had spotted previously and which had excellent reviews. There was plenty of seating outside but unfortunately, again, also several people exhaling clouds of smoke into the early morning sunshine. The only available indoor seating area, where, even in France, smoking is not allowed, was in a small backroom next to the toilet. We took a seat there and ordered. The owner seemed amused by our choice of seating but we were happy enough in our cloistered spot.

Left alone we enjoyed a delicious cappuccino and kept ourselves entertained studying the numerous sacks of coffee scattered around what was more of a storeroom than a customer seating area. We went back to this café frequently, always passing Da Laura's and hoping they would see us and wonder why we had deserted them.

Overjoyed at arrival of cappuccino

TRACY – FRENCH BUREAUCRACY

It had taken a little over a year for Les to get his pension sorted before we departed France for Australia in 2018. Witnessing the rigmarole he had gone through, I did what I could to get my pension administration in order before I left France. Being a child-bride, I still had many years left before I could access my contributions. I was pleased I could obtain online access to my pension, pre-departure. At some point, however, soon after we left France, I was shut out of the system and it was impossible to reset my password. Knowing the challenge of French bureaucracy, we had set aside a day to visit the retirement office (CARSAT).

The administration had done their best to hide the office on the second floor of a grubby shopping complex, with no signage. The sales assistant in a nearby sporting store begrudgingly pointed the way. Couldn't blame her as I could see that others following me in were also asking for directions. We climbed the two sets of stairs and could see

20 others gathering in front of a non-descript doorway. A man emerged through the portal and we could see that there were a dozen others already inside.

Avez-vous pris rendez-vous ? Have you made an appointment? he asked.

Ce n'est pas possible. It's not possible came a reply from the chorus. The man shrugged his shoulders and exited down the stairs. At this point, I noticed a small poster that said,

'12 mois avant, je prepare ma retraite! …Demandez votre retraite en ligne! C'est simple, facile et securise!' Prepare for your retirement 12 months in advance. Ask for your retirement information on line. It's simple, easy and secure!

Lie. Lie. Lie. As my 12 months in advance period was still years away, we abandoned all hope of receiving a favourable reception, and left.

LES – THE OTHER CANNES

Finally, a reasonable night's sleep. The jetlag was wearing off at last. I awoke at 6am refreshed and ready to face the day and started with a stroll into town. I've always enjoyed getting out when most other people are still sleeping, and watching a town wake up. The street cleaners were out in force, pressure spraying the streets and collecting the various objects left by the previous night's revellers. I walked along the Croisette and took a few pictures of the five-star hotels across the street, idly wondering if anyone might be looking out of their window and watching me. It seemed an unlikely scenario. I took more pictures, this time of some ridiculously overpriced clothing items (there was no price tag, I just assumed they would be overpriced). The famous Cannes Croisette has always struck me as the classic facade, walk a few streets back towards the station, and it looks like any other town with quaint, scruffy streets, shops and restaurants that normal people might actually shop or dine in.

Classic Cannes panorama

Bus station, Cannes

TRACY – SOJOURN TO SOPHIA ANTIPOLIS

Les loves train travel. If he had his way, instead of flying to France he would have flown to Singapore and then caught the train, up through Malaysia and Thailand to China where he would have connected with the Trans-Siberian, or Trans Mongolian Express across the Steppes to Europe. He would of course, have been doing this on his own as I'm not an enthusiast of shared public toilets that accompany long rail journeys. So, as a compromise, this trip had lots of rail travel for relatively brief trips. The journey that kisses the Mediterranean Coast from Cannes to Ventimiglia in Italy is a favourite, even though we are warned over the public announcement system to beware, as there are thieves currently operating on the train. I find everything interesting: from the sparkling, azure water to the craggy rocks and the vivid graffiti. Sun worshipers have colourful towels strewn upon the often-pebbly shores, and I never tire of hearing children's screeches of delight as they splash into the water. I also love the orangey, pink and yellow-hued houses we fly past, whose colours look more beautiful as they soften each year in the ever-present sunshine.

We rendezvoused with a friend at the deserted Biot station, which is a stone's throw from the better known and bustling Antibes. She drove us inland and up the winding back roads to Sophia Antipolis which is a 2,400-hectare Technopole (business park). We had worked with Amadeus for a decade before moving to Thailand in 2007. It's a beautiful area and I loved listening to the chorus of noisy cicadas as we made our ascent. Lunch was at a friend's restaurant called Ma Dame Nova. The midday meal is an important institution in French life, something I came to appreciate during my time here. I enjoyed an exotic salad, and Les ordered a hamburger. He crossed his fingers that the meat would be well cooked, a rarity in France, with this request often met in restaurants with disdain. (Side note: It was well-cooked and delicious).

We returned to our apartment in Cannes to settle in for the evening watching the Trooping of the Colour in London on the BBC. The Queen looked well, smiling broadly from the palace balcony on this platinum jubilee. I notice that she now leans on a cane, but she continues to be amazing for someone of her advanced vintage.

LES – DAY TRIP TO ITALY

We were keen to do some cycling and had planned to rent bikes from a local shop and head along the coast to Antibes and beyond. But, after some discussion, we decided that, due to inclement weather, we would just take the train to Antibes, mooch about and possibly, if the rain held off, rent bikes there. We had originally planned a lengthier train trip of the better part of ninety minutes to Ventimiglia, just across the Italian border, followed by a bus to Dolceacqua, a quaint and, until recently, undiscovered gem of the Italian Riviera, although it's not actually on the coast. We delayed this adventure until the sun reappeared.

I had discovered, on a recent train ticket buying expedition, that SNCF, the French train company, had not updated their automated machines since the 1990s. Also, in most stations only around half of them actually work. I realised it was time to get with the scene and downloaded their app so that I could book the tickets on my phone.

. . .

All went well until it came time to pay. I discovered that our bank, because of a mix up the previous day, had blocked my French credit card. I couldn't use my Australian one online due to security requirements to send a text message to the phones we weren't using, so we went to the station and jumped through the required hoops to buy the tickets there. An uneventful day in Antibes followed. The bike hiring didn't happen.

TRACY – UNWELCOME MESSAGE

We were distracted the following morning, having received a WhatsApp note from our sister-in-law in London alerting us that our nephew had caught COVID and that this had thrown his travel plans back to Hong Kong into question. We were two weeks away from arriving in the UK, and we reviewed alternate accommodation arrangements in the event that COVID was still in the household when we arrived. Catching COVID anywhere was an outcome we knew was possible when we booked our flights. I particularly didn't want to catch COVID at the writers' conference I was attending at the end of June, and just before I was flying home to Brisbane. I knew a hall full of people was a likely place for infection.

We caught up with good friends at the Okey beachside restaurant in Cannes. The location is stunning, looking across the Mediterranean to the Esterel mountains. Many sun-worshipers had hired deck chairs on a temporary pier raised high over the water. This depicted the typical scene that millions imagine when they think of the French Riviera.

Sunseekers at Okey beach, Cannes

TRACY – MOANS IN THE MORNING.

We heard the most terrible sounds this morning – like a guttural cry for help from olden times when the undertaker was calling out, 'bring out your dead'. We debated whether it was a cat or indeed a human in pain. I recorded the sounds on my phone in case I needed to provide evidence to the police. A further investigation identified an enormous seagull who had caught a rat and was trying to keep it for themselves, away from other prying birds.

As I write this, Les is attempting to purchase our morning train tickets over the internet. It seems possible that, having gone to the trouble of using an online site to order them, we need to collect a physical ticket. He's not happy.

LES – ANDIAMO

Having wasted an hour or more on the phone trying to sort out a suspected credit card bungle, we made our way to the station again, determined to enjoy a day in Italy. We still intended to fulfil our plan to take the train to the border town of Ventimiglia and then a local bus to our favourite village of Dolceacqua a few miles inland. We enjoyed the picturesque train journey along the coast and arrived in Ventimiglia ready to sample a cappuccino or two.

Tracy had googled the best place for coffee and we set off to *Café Vergera*, a few minutes' walk from the station. We enjoyed a late breakfast at around 30% of what we would have paid for a far inferior one in Cannes. This experience reminded me of one of my favourite self-penned aphorisms, *one of the best things about living in France is that it is close to Italy.* We then walked to the bike shop where we hoped to rent bikes and ride the eleven kilometres to Dolceacqua - the idea of taking the bus had dissipated somewhere along the way and anyway, buying bus tickets in Italy had stumped us before as they seldom seem to actually sell them on the bus. We entered the bike shop and were greeted by a lugubrious fellow called Luigi, the bike shop owner. He spoke a bit of French but, like most Italians, also spoke the language of the hands.

In a mixture of French, Italian, English and hand gestures, I negotiated the rental of two serviceable, but slightly dilapidated looking, bikes. It was just after 10am and we only wanted the bikes for four hours so that we could ride to Dolceacqua, have a leisurely lunch, and then return them around 2pm. Unfortunately for us, Luigi had other plans. Being a bike shop owner, he was, of course, also an avid cyclist and told us he had planned a ride with friends at midday so we would need to have the bikes back by then, or, keep them 'til 4 pm when the shop would re-open. We wanted to be on our way home by then, so we agreed to ensure we were back by midday to allow him to join his *amigi*.

After some saddle adjusting, we pedalled off in the direction of Dolceacqua, keeping an eye out for wayward Italian drivers who may have felt it was their duty to knock a couple of overweight foreign cyclists off their *bici*. We found the turn for Dolceacqua with no problem but then remembered that on a previous visit we had discovered a newly built bike path which avoided the hilly main road altogether. We could actually see the path on the other side of the dried-up river bed. However, there was no way to access it from the main road until, a kilometre or so further along, we came upon a turnoff which seemed to lead toward the ever-beckoning bike path. We rode down the small road but soon became lost in some kind of industrial site and quickly gave up. As we rode back along the main road, I discovered an access way to the bike track but Tracy was too far ahead to hear my exhortations to join me and so I gave up and followed her back towards the coast road.

Abandoning our Dolceaqua plan, we had somehow forgotten it involved climbing a steep hill, which we were not keen to do on the borrowed bikes, we joined another newly built bike path which followed the coast and went through the small Italian Riviera resort towns of Vallecrosia and Bordighera. This was a flat road, but there was a strong headwind and after forty minutes, we'd had enough fun for one day and turned around to make our way back to Luigi's place to return the bikes.

The track took a few twists and turns eventually leading us back to the main road less than a kilometre from the affable Italian's shop. In fact, we realised in retrospect, as one always does, that we could have avoided the busy main road altogether and used the brightly painted, car free, bike track for around 95% of our trip. Next time.

Luigi was very pleased to see us, saying "fast" in his best English. We tried to explain we had failed in our mission to reach Dolceaqua, and discussed, again in a variety of languages and gestures, where we had been and what we had discovered of his small area of Italy. This proved too complicated and we resorted to discussing a far simpler subject, food. Luigi recommended a restaurant amusingly called *Pasta Basta,* which roughly translates as *Enough Pasta* - not *Bastard Pasta* as some of you may be thinking.

Luigi explains lunch options

TRACY – THEOULE SUR MER

Enjoyed our mini-Italian adventure yesterday combining train travel, cycling and delicious coffee. Pleased that we avoided a minor marital skirmish when I sped ahead on my cycle and didn't hear my husband's exhortations to turn left. We also enjoyed a coffee and train journey as we visited our favourite beach at Theoule sur Mer. It's a sleepy village cradled at the foot of the Esterels. The ride along the coast to Frejus is popular with cyclists, providing amazing views and a few steep ascents and scary descents.

Les – A visit to the scene of a book cover

When we lived in Mandelieu, apart from futile trips to Cannes in search of good coffee, we often used to venture west along the coast to another small town, Theoule sur Mer. There wasn't much at Theoule but there was a lovely, not much used, beach which we liked. In fact, we liked it so much that it was featured on the cover of my book, *My Brother's Bicycle*. We studied the timetable and took the train to Theoule for another walk down memory lane. Nothing much had changed although the local council had spent a bit of money upgrading some of the coastal paths which abound in this region and we had a relaxing stroll around the town.

We planned to take the bus back, as the vagaries of the SNCF train schedule were of little use, especially as it was a Sunday. The bus did not operate with any great level of frequency either, but there was one scheduled which we thought would suit our timings. However, after discovering that our favourite coffee shop in Theoule was closed, and there was little else to do, we realised that we still had the better part of forty minutes to wait for the bus. So, we walked.

We had no intention of walking the entire way back to Cannes but knew, having ridden this route many times previously, there was a picturesque, if hilly, route along the coast back to La Napoule, where we could catch the bus. We timed it perfectly and after just a few minutes wait at the bus stop, where we engaged in convivial conversation with an English couple also waiting, we boarded a small, but well air-conditioned bus which took us along the coast in the direction of Cannes. Buses rarely take the most direct route and this one was no different. After a few kilometres of driving along the coast, it veered off the main road and took us down some charming back streets. A few minutes later we re-joined the coast road and continued towards Cannes, with the red, rocky escarpments of Cannes La Bocca on our left, and the glistening Mediterranean on our right.

Favourite beach at Theoule sur Mer

TRACY – BACK TO THE BANK IN CANNES

The following day, we visited to the bank. This was becoming a daily occurrence. There was as usual, a long queue at the door. Lots of cranky foreigners and a few dogs on leads. Upon checking with reception, they confirmed that our cards had not arrived. *'Did you bring your cheque book with you?' they asked.* We looked at each other and a smile flitted across our faces. We thought we were now starring in an episode of Back to the Future. A special one-off withdrawal was arranged and we left with 600 euros.

Les – A battle with the bank

The complications caused by no longer having a usable French credit card continued. We were unable to use our Australian one easily as validation was being sent to our Australian phone number and we had temporary SIM cards while we were in Europe. All of this combined to make any online purchase of train tickets almost impossible. So, we had to resort to using cash.

Long gone are the days of humans providing any valued service. There was a ticket office at the station but it operated on a particularly unhelpful schedule. There were only one or two machines that allowed payment in cash, and these had an alarming propensity to be out of order. What to do? We threw caution to the wind, adopted criminal like behaviour and boarded the train to Antibes - without a ticket. The excitement was palpable as we sat on the train for the ten-minute journey, expecting at any second to be arrested for fare avoidance. I've never felt so alive.

TRACY – OLD ANTIBES

Antibes-Juan Les Pins is one of the well-known towns on the Riviera. We lived on the Cap d'Antibes, cradled between these two resort locations, when we first arrived in 1997. The old town in Antibes is one of the most charming on the Cote d'Azur, surrounded by impressive ramparts providing a spectacular platform from which to survey the sparkling super-yachts and the sun worshipers on the Plage de la Gravette.

You can then stroll through the aromatic Marché Provençal on Cours Masséna enjoying the sensory delights of the dried lavender and freshly cut flowers. On a Saturday morning, there is often laughter as wedding parties emerge from the local *Mairie* (town hall). Old Antibes is a wonderful place to get lost in as you navigate the narrow cobbled-alleys. If you're lucky, you'll stumble upon one of our favourite cafés called Choopys, serving excellent cappuccinos and mouth-watering muffins in a cosy environment.

Old Antibes street scene

Under the ramparts in Antibes

One of the best outcomes for us on this day in Antibes was that the machine accepting cash at the railway station was working. We patiently turned the many dials, that would have been at home on Doctor Who's Tardis, and stocked up on tickets for the coming days. Our criminal days were behind us, for now.

LES – TO BANK OR NOT TO BANK

We tackled the bank again today, this time in person. We'd been annoyingly upsold to new "more secure" bank cards which we didn't need, but when we had been to collect them the previous week, they weren't ready. No real surprise there, *c'est comme ça*, but, unbeknownst to us, the lady who checked their arrival for us had also cancelled the existing cards. Of course, I didn't realise this until later that day when I tried to buy some train tickets and the card was refused. Assuming this was just a glitch on the SNCF website, we had gone to the station but could not use the card there either. Our suspicions were confirmed when we also tried using them at the ATM of the issuing bank itself. Great, it was now late on a Friday afternoon, so of course we could do nothing before the following week and, to make matters worse, the following Monday was a public holiday. In reality, our plight was not so awful. We had cash and we also had access to our Australian account so we weren't about to starve. It was, however, frustrating in the extreme.

. . .

Back to the bank experience. Following the long weekend, which we survived unscathed, despite out penurious situation, we arrived at the bank bright and early on Tuesday morning, a few minutes before opening time. A long queue had already formed. A raggle-taggle band of backpackers, cruise takers and older locals, some of whom were accompanied by scraggly looking dogs. Some of the dogs were on leads, but most were free to snuffle around, occasionally licking an unsuspecting person's foot, an act which was studiously ignored by its owner. At precisely 09.30, the automatic door slid open and we all shuffled slowly forwards to determine our fate. I idly wondered why so many French people had been allowed in to what, I thought, was a branch specifically for foreigners - which translates wonderfully into French as *étranger*. Our visit turned out to be as futile as I had always known it would be. There was no sign of the new cards and no solution to the problem was offered, despite our remonstrations with the unresponsive staff. The only solution they offered was to withdraw cash with a temporary card. We had no choice but to meekly accept this and resign ourselves to return another day.

Following our experience with French bureaucracy, Tracy took the train to Antibes to meet a friend while I returned to our rented apartment, took a shower and lay down on the bed to recover my strength. I stayed in this position for most of the day, dozing and reading. Speaking a foreign language and trying to be assertive is an exhausting business.

. . .

That evening we watched a couple of episodes of the wonderful Danish political drama *Borgen*. This show is set in Copenhagen and revolves around the machinations of a female politician. I enjoyed trying to understand the language and occasionally glimpse somewhere I recognised from the year I spent in the city in the early 80s.

This was followed by yet another early night. A few hours later, we were woken by loud explosions and feared the worst. Had the Italians finally invaded? After a few minutes we realised it was just fireworks, although we could not imagine the occasion. It wasn't July 14th. The flashes and explosions went on for about twenty minutes, before finally ceasing at around 11.30 pm and we tried to go back to sleep. It was a sultry night and even with two fans wafting air across our supine bodies, we tossed and turned fitfully. The next morning, we discovered that the fireworks had been part of an Indian wedding celebration. So not French at all, but we still blamed them.

But the hot, noisy night was to be nothing compared to the experiences of the following day. What follows are two accounts. A real tale of two cities, or in our case, two bureaucracies.

TRACY – OH JOY OH JOY

On the morning walk to the beach in Cannes, we spotted a trade show for retired people and those approaching retirement. Oh Joy Oh Joy. Would I be able to find someone to help me access my retirement account again? It was 9.45am and after wandering around we found a stall with a woman from CARSAT. There was no queue and she smiled when I approached the table. A double win. I was able to show her my social security number and Carte Vitale, and within ten minutes I was able to access online, my retirement account. So excited and relieved. A trip to France twelve months before my retirement may now no longer be necessary.

And then we went to the bank. If only our earlier success could be repeated. We took seats inside and waited patiently to be called. While we waited, we chatted with an elderly Irish lady and her son who were there to sort out a vaguely described, monthly deduction of a hundred euros from her account, that was somehow related to

Brexit. It was reassuring to know that there were others battling bureaucracy.

After thirty minutes, we finally met our account manager. The cards had arrived but one of the staff had accidentally cut the corner off mine when she opened the envelope. "It will be fine," we told me. Still, I was able to activate it using my current PIN while Les used his existing PIN and was not. At least we had one working card for our European holiday, we thought. Which we did, until it was swallowed a week later by an ATM in Sutton, which I believe took exception to the missing corner of the card. We'll never know.

LES – A SURPRISING BUREAUCRATIC SUCCESS

A few months before we left Australia for France, Tracy had realised that she no longer had access to the details of her upcoming French pension. The French don't easily deal with the concept that not everyone lives in France. She had sent a letter to no avail. On this trip, a few days previously, we had bravely attempted to visit the *retraite* offices, but, on arrival, were firmly told we could not see anyone without an appointment. "Fair enough," we said, "can we make one?" *Non.*

So, imagine our amazement and delight when, as we strolled through the early morning sunshine on our way, once again to the bank, we came across a special presentation display set up specifically to assist people with retirement. We found the relevant counter and spoke to a particularly friendly lady who, once provided with Tracy's social security number and date of birth, accessed her account on her mobile phone, and set up a new login and password. The whole encounter took no more than ten

Les – A surprising bureaucratic success

minutes. Incredible. If only the bank were at least half as efficient.

On an achievement high, we continued on to the bank. We entered and told them we had an appointment with our counsellor. A moment later, she appeared smiling and waving two new bank cards which had finally arrived. It seemed this was going to be our lucky day. The euphoria was short-lived. As I tried to validate my card with the PIN I had been using for the past twenty-five years, I found that it did not work.

The bank assured me they had not changed it but this was the only real answer. Obviously, the complete bozo, who a few days earlier, when we enquired whether the new cards had arrived, had clicked some option which cancelled the old ones. This, I realised, was the reason we had not been able to use them since then. Additionally, it was clear to me now, she had also selected an option to change my PIN, even though this was the last thing I wanted.

All of this was, of course, strenuously denied by everyone, as was the simple task of reinstating the old cards. It was all *impossible*. Fortunately, Tracy's card worked and I realised the only, albeit temporary, solution was to defy all the known laws of security by using it for the remainder of my trip. After which, we would tell the bank we did not need the new, biometric, more expensive cards which I did not want in the first place. The final straw in this sorry saga of inefficiency was that Tracy's card, the only one that worked, had the corner cut off by an over exuberant mail opener, narrowly missing the all-important biometric chip.

In the evening, I joined another friend of mine, an ex-colleague, for dinner and drinks, too many drinks as it transpired, by the port in Golfe Juan. She shared her stories of a distant past when I had worked for the same company as her. I listened to her tales of poor management and eccentric colleagues with a strange mix of envy; that I did not still work there, and joy; that I did not still work there.

A restless, thirsty night followed, caused by the consumption of too much wine the night before. I planned a quiet day. We abandoned plans for another trip to Italy and, after a cappuccino in our favourite café, spent the day dozing, watching TV and generally doing very little. Another early night beckoned.

The day was not completely wasted. We did some planning for our impending few days in Paris. Plans were not complex - a visit to the Musee d'Orsay and a few hours following in the footsteps of Henry Miller around Montparnasse. Some of it happened.

TRACY – DAY TRIP TO NICE

Nice is a colourful and lively city and a UNESCO listed World Heritage site. It's the fifth largest in France located thirty kilometres from Monaco and forty kilometres from the Italian border, and a decent cup of coffee. The city has a charming port, busy international airport and a wonderful seven-kilometre boardwalk along the seafront called the Promenade des Anglais, attracting runners, cyclists, rollerbladers, scooterers, Segwayers and pedestrians. Yes, it is a busy place. There is, of course, also a long beach, but make sure you have sturdy sandals with you for navigating the path to the water over the problematic pebbles. Away from the seafront, there are a diversity of markets including antique and flea markets known as *Puces de Nice*, flower, food and fish markets. It's a great place for strolling and sitting at a café, watching life pass by as you soak in the sunshine. If you visit during the middle of the day as we were, you will hear a loud boom. It occurs every day at 12.00 and has been doing so since 1861. There's a charming story behind this shared by Margo Lestz on

. . .

https://thegoodlifefrance.com/history-nice-midday-cannon/

It was 1861, it was lunchtime and Thomas Coventry-More was hungry. This Scottish Lord (let's call him Tom) and his wife were spending their winter in Nice, as usual, and the missus was late coming home for lunch, as usual.

Every morning she would go out for a stroll, meet other British ladies, and spend hours gossiping about who was doing what on the French Riviera. She often forgot all about having lunch with her poor husband, who was sitting at home waiting for her.

Tom was an ex-British army officer and a punctual man. He wanted to eat lunch at the specified hour and not one minute later. But he was also a problem-solver, so he set out to solve this one. He thought about his army experiences and in no time, he had a plan. A perfectly simple plan. He went to the Nice city council, since he needed their cooperation, and explained his idea.

To make sure they had understood his Scottish accent, they repeated his proposition: "you want us to go to the top of the hill every day at noon and shoot off a cannon, which will surely frighten our citizens, just to remind your wife to come home for lunch?"

"Yes, that's it, old chap, you've understood perfectly. Of course, since it is mainly for my benefit, I will pay all the costs and I even have an old cannon lying around that I will donate for the task."

The council huddled together to make their decision.

"These English are crazy (to the French all British are English – even if they are Scottish). Yes, they are crazy, but he is going to pay... It will frighten people at first, but then the Niçois (people of Nice) will get used to it, and it will only frighten tourists. That could be fun."

"Well, yes, why not?" they answered.

All went along very well like this for years until finally Tom and his wife stopped coming to Nice. Since he was no longer footing the bill for the firing of the cannon, the council stopped doing it. Havoc must have ensued in Nice, as by now everyone had become used to the noon signal.

Many people were late for lunch, and some even missed it altogether – all because there was no cannon fire to remind them.

'Well, this was just not acceptable and the council had to reinstate the midday signal'.

Today it is no longer a cannon that is heard, but a firework. It is still set off manually each day at noon and now the Niçois never miss their lunch!

On the Promenade des Anglais

Les – It's all Greek to me

Nice, of course, is the best known of the towns along the Riviera, perhaps vying with Cannes. The area around Nice has been populated by man for about 400,000 years, according to archaeological evidence. From the 4th century BC, the Phocaean Greeks established a town here named Nikaia, after the Greek goddess of victory, Nike. Over time, the pronunciation has changed to what we hear now. It didn't become part of France until 1860, when it was handed over as part of the Treaty of Turin.

Nice was a town we had visited many times in the past and it seemed only fitting that we venture there again. We found fast trains in both directions, which was a definite plus. Stopping at all the small provincial stations along the way becomes a trifle boring after a while.

When we returned to Cannes, we spent an enjoyable afternoon with friends in our new favourite restaurant, La Piazza.

We had tried taking a table at another establishment, but the fellow who greeted us had the air of the recently bereaved. He was the most miserable, unfriendly and unwelcoming person I have met in many a year. There were four of us; two wanted to eat and two didn't. This did not meet with his strict, "this is a restaurant, you have to eat," policy. The place was empty and it wasn't as if we had bought our own sandwiches. We left him to his sad life and went elsewhere. I vented my spleen a few hours later by giving his place a 1-star review on Google. That'll teach him.

LES - A LUCKY ESCAPE

I visited a friend for lunch today. I'd first met him at a work function where our multinational company was celebrating its eclectic mix of nationalities. We'd ended up standing next to each other for a group photo, being taken by the main building entrance, just as someone who had interviewed, and turned me down, for a job returned from lunch. "You had a lucky escape", he muttered and I knew we would get along.

Over the years I made many friends where I worked. I remember some characters more than others. There was the fellow who managed the training team I eventually joined. He'd impressed me at a presentation to some clients when, demonstrating the flexibility of our travel booking system he booked a flight for a Mr M. Jackson. Then to show how other names could be easily added he said, in his wonderful French accent, "And, of course, Michael is travelling with his little friend" and proceeded to add a child to the booking. Political incorrectness at its best.

And there was a chap who I worked with for a while when I first joined. I was keen to learn the language and he and I would go off at lunchtime in his Citroen and I would try to speak French. His driving was typically French and he had the wonderful habit of saying "Ooplah" every time he narrowly avoided an accident. I still say this whenever I drop, or nearly drop, anything.

In the evening we headed for the town of Mouans Sartoux by train to meet some other friends I had worked with more recently. The café we had arranged to meet in was only five hundred metres from the station but of course we got lost in the maze of small streets. We eventually found the square, where we had arranged to meet, one of many, and took a seat while we waited for our friends to arrive. They eventually turned up about thirty minutes late having been at an entirely different establishment across the square. "Oh, we thought you'd see us," they said.

LES – ONCE MORE, DOWN TO THE BEACH

Tracy had made plans to meet up with a friend of hers, who had the capacity to deprive donkeys of a hind leg, so I stayed home alone. I was reminded of a George Bernard Shaw quote, "she had lost the art of conversation but unfortunately not the power of speech".

After an hour or so enjoying my seclusion, I ventured out, planning to visit a small park I had spotted nearby which had been closed. It was only a few minutes' walk from our lodging and I was soon strolling through the peaceful scenery there. I felt the need for a call of nature and was pleasantly surprised to find a public toilet with all the accoutrements required for a successful visit. I then walked back towards town trying to avoid the complete descent, as I had no desire to clamber uphill again in the middle of the day. An hour or so later Tracy arrived home with her ears intact, although I got the distinct feeling that one leg was shorter than the other.

TRACY – ILE SAINTE MARGUERITE

A short ferry ride away from bustling Cannes, are the Îles de Lérins comprising Île Sainte-Marguerite and Île Saint-Honorat. I visited the larger Ile Sainte Marguerite for three reasons. Firstly, because it has a tranquil forest of pines and eucalyptus trees, planted at the beginning of the 19th century. Perfect for strolling through while enjoying a backdrop of humming cicadas. Secondly, because local authorities have created an underwater eco-museum called Écomusée sous-marin, which I was keen to explore. This new attraction features a series of six monumental, three-dimensional portraits of local members of the community, covering a range of ages and professions. For example, one sculpture is of Maurice, an 80-year-old local fisherman, and another of Anouk, a 9-year-old primary school student. And the third reason was because there was a spot on the island, not too far from the royal fort, where a famous and unidentified man had been held captive centuries before and forced to wear an iron mask, where I had staged another dramatic event.

The event had royal implications and was described in a novel I had written under my pen name, Jane Ellyson.

I was able to achieve Objective One and Three but struggled with number Two. While the water was crystal clear, getting out to the snorkelling spot required wading through shallow water on slimy moss-covered rocks. I attempted the manoeuvre several times, each time wondering how long it would take for someone to find me if I slipped and broke my back. I gave up and retired to a fallen log where I soaked up the sun's delicious rays while watching others on small watercraft seamlessly slip into the water from a less hazardous departure point.

Between Ile Sainte Marguerite and Saint Honorat in the Illes des Lerins

Les – Avoiding boats and queues

I stayed home again while Tracy ventured out to the islands off the coast. I try to avoid boats and queuing. In the evening, we met up with another old colleague who entertained us with stories of her impending divorce.

An early night, for a change, as we leave tomorrow for Paris.

TRACY – DEPARTING FOR PARIS BY TGV

We had an early morning departure by train from Cannes. Quietly descending the two floors of stairs from our apartment to street level with our heavy bags was *mission impossible*. Still, we knew we would no longer be there to cop the inevitable wrath of our neighbours. It embarrassed me how noisy our bags were as the wheels turned on the uneven concrete path, in the stillness of the early morning.

We were staying in a friend's apartment in Paris and had already been warned that their neighbours would be knocking on the door as soon as we arrived to let us know they could hear us moving about the apartment.

We had been planning our time in Paris and intended to spend a day visiting cafés, cemeteries and other locales frequented by writer Henry Miller. Les' writing is hugely influenced by Henry Miller along with Dostoievsky and Kafka – or so he likes to think.

Les – On the train to Paris

A restless night, as always, before an early start. At 5am an unremitting cacophony emanated from my phone. I struggled to make it stop as it grew ever louder, no doubt disturbing, not only me, but also our noise-sensitive neighbours. We had warned them we had an early start, but I was relieved when I finally managed to switch the alarm off.

We left the apartment and struggled down the hill with our luggage, towards the station, at every minute at risk of being crushed by our overweight bags. The route we had meticulously planned over the past few days, was blocked by council workers who had chosen that particular morning, to make an early start on some, obviously highly important, hedge cutting. We were forced to take a deviation along the recently cleaned, and therefore, still wet and slippery pavements and continued on our way.

Our best laid plans for boarding the train were also thrown into confusion when we were informed that Coach 1 was not at the front of the train but bizarrely at the very back. Also, in a splendid display of French logic, the various parts of the platform were not marked numerically but alphabetically. So, 1 became Z. I realised later that this was related to carriage 1 being the front of the train when it left Paris but, as it was unable to turn around at its destination of Nice, the carriage order was reversed for the return trip. It seemed that the simple act of renumbering the carriages for each leg of the journey had not occurred to anyone at SNCF.

We enjoyed the journey as the TGV plummeted through the French countryside and arrived in Paris a few minutes early. Once we had negotiated the melee at the station and found the taxi rank, we arrived safely at our accommodation. We climbed possibly the ricketiest set of stairs I have ever encountered, and entered the tiny but well-appointed apartment. A lovely day strolling the streets followed, and we wished we had planned a longer stay in one of Europe's most beautiful cities.

Tracy – Arriving in Paris

Les spent a significant amount of time muttering about the need for SNCF to improve the way they number their carriages. Having found our seats, we settled in for the five-hour journey. The first hour or so along the coast was lovely. Snatches of aqua-marine sea were revealed behind the red rocks of the Esterels. I put my earphones in to listen to an audible book and immediately started drifting in and out of sleep. When I woke, I was intrigued to see around 30 wind turbines near the railway lines. I thought they were impressive. I was pleased with the sandwiches that Les had insisted we purchase the day before. (He'll be smiling as he reads this).

The train started slowing as we entered the city limits. I've always been nervous about arriving at Gare de Lyon as the result of a dodgy ticket scam I experienced 30 years previously. Even today you can see shady characters scanning arrivals for disoriented travellers, who they could *assist.*

I'm pleased that we had agreed beforehand that we would take a taxi, even though there was a very long, slow-moving, snaking queue of other passengers with the same intention. In the relative safety of the line, I could relax and survey my surroundings. Signs everywhere warned travellers about taking unregistered taxis. A dodgy character was regularly walking the line to encourage impatient travellers to skip the queue and come with him. Not a single traveller moved. I was pleased. There was a charming gentleman of African origin managing the front of the queue who wished us well when we finally climbed into our taxi. Safe inside, I could finally relax and enjoy looking out the window at the imposing buildings, creative street signs and manic delivery drivers zig-zagging across traffic lanes.

We'd been told that the apartment was small and to be entered via a narrow, blue staircase. Both statements were accurate. We had thought that the last of our days of lugging suitcases upstairs were behind us. Delighted that we could achieve this feat without damaging the stairs or our backs, we ventured out toward the Musée d'Orsay.

Upon arrival at the museum, Les immediately dismissed the idea of going in when he saw the length of the queue. He's had enough of queuing, which is synonymous, or part and parcel, of visiting any place of notoriety anywhere in the world. I proposed a stroll down to nearby St Germain des Pres, where we stopped for coffee at an enticing café called *Aux Vieux Garçons*. At €7.00 a cup, it was our most expensive cappuccino come viennois coffee to date.

Les at his namesake cafe (Aux Vieux Garçons)
loosely translated as The Old Boys' Place

However, it was not as expensive as nearby *Les Deux Magots* where a cappuccino would set you back €8.00. But then you were really not paying for the coffee as much as the opportunity to sit on the sidewalk at this famous landmark. Further strolling and snapping of photos, then back to the apartment after a visit to FranPrix, a local supermarket, to buy wine, cheese, milk and cereal.

Les – In Paris

We were quite the tourists today. Tracy wanted to explore the Canal St Martin area so we found our way there and ambled around for a while thinking we were in Amsterdam, with bikes and canals everywhere. We had a couple of what passes for a cappuccino in Paris at a local bar, this time paying far less than we had in the trendy St Germain area.

Then we walked to The Sacre Coeur. Forty minutes, said Google maps. But of course, as everybody who's ever been there knows, at least thirty-eight of those minutes are uphill, the last twenty-nine being almost Everest like in their *dénivellement*. But we made it and, avoiding the ubiquitous sellers of tat who hang around at the entrance, went into the building itself just before 11am. This coincided with Matins. A superfluity of nuns was breaking into song just as we went in. A few minutes later, a trio of clerics came on stage, praising the Lord. I'm always intrigued by the pious, especially if they appear intelligent. They praise the creator for his munificent acts, yet seem to ignore all the destructive ones. *What a shame no-*

one is listening to your supplications, I thought. Not wanting to encourage them in their delusion, I didn't take any photos even though the inside of the building is spectacular.

Our next stop was an English bookshop where Tracy had arranged to call in and leave a copy of one of her books, *Substitute Child*, an action-adventure story with a touch of romance, which has scenes in the city of love, of course.

After that, we met up with an old friend who had moved to Paris. She hadn't changed much although I was surprised how much more English she sounded than when I first met her.

Exhausted after so much walking, we returned to our apartment to rest, planning to investigate a local park later that evening. It didn't happen.

Sacre Coeur, the ascent

LES – SEARCHING FOR HENRY MILLER

Last night was another tropical night with little respite from the heat. I slept fitfully and was happy to see the grey light of dawn. We started the day at Montparnasse cemetery where several high-profile artists, writers and musicians are buried. Despite the hi-tech option, at the entrance, of a downloadable map, I was still only able to locate the last resting place of Jean-Paul Sartre and Simone de Beauvoir. I searched in vain for the grave of Guy de Maupassant but, after a few minutes, gave up and we moved on to the next part of our literary trail - following, in part at least, in the steps of Henry Miller. Henry had, along with several other writers, spent much of his time eating, drinking and I suppose writing, at various bars and restaurants in the area. I'm sure Blvd Raspail, in Henry's day, was less busy, but we battled with the traffic and frequent ambulance and police sirens before finding one of his old haunts - La Rotunda. There was a small Italian café called Villa Borghese across the road. It reminded me of the first line of Henry's first book, Tropic of Cancer - *I am living in the Villa Borghese*. Intrigued, I had to cross the road and have a coffee. I knew there was probably no genuine connection, in fact, as the owner was Italian it was most likely a simple coincidence, but who knows?

I then went a little further along Blvd Raspail to the Tschann bookshop where Henry's books were first sold, but there was no sign of them anywhere. I inquired of the feckless youth at the counter, but he showed little enthusiasm for my question. *How are the mighty fallen?* I thought as I left the shop.

I figured that was enough literary searching for one day and we continued with an exploratory trip to Gare du Nord where we will take the train to London.

In the evening, I inveigled Tracy out for a Happy Hour drink. This is a new concept in France, presumably instigated in an effort to attract customers after the three years or so of COVID. Most bars sell beer and a variety of other beverages at bargain prices between the hours of 3 or 4pm until around 7pm. Some go as far as having it until 11pm during the week. We went to a place where we had had lunch on the previous two days. We sat looking at the traffic and marvelling at the lack of accidents while we enjoyed our drinks.

When it came time to pay, I approached the bar. At that early evening hour, despite the cheap drinks, we were pretty much the only customers, but the guy who had served us was outside chatting to the only other customers. I waited patiently at the bar, but he showed no signs of coming inside. There was an older gentleman sitting at a table next to the bar who resembled the waiter and who I assumed was his father. He studiously ignored me, seeming to be entirely transfixed by some paperwork. After a while, I ventured outside and waved my bankcard in the direction of the guy who had served us, asking if I could pay. He pointed at the older fellow, who was still concentrating on his paperwork. I went back inside, only to be ignored again. I mustered my language skills and like to think I said something like *any danger of me paying?* Dad slowly got to his feet, sighing almost imperceptibly, and lumbered to a position behind the bar where he could reach the till. He pressed a few buttons and mumbled a number, proffering the payment machine vaguely in my direction. I paid and didn't leave a tip.

We walked slowly home. Tracy has a low tolerance for alcohol and had, as ever, underestimated the content of the drink she had ordered, and quaffed as if it were lemonade. Back at the apartment, we gorged ourselves on snacks we had purchased and settled down for the evening.

Tracy – In the footsteps of Henry Miller

We had difficulty sleeping last night. There was too much light and I scrambled for an eye mask, but it didn't help. My husband said I made piglet impressions most of the night, which is his subtle way of saying I was snoring. A slow rise this morning.

First thing. We traced our steps from our apartment to Gare de Nord via the metro, counting the steps on each stairway and imagining how easy, or not, it would be to come this way, with our luggage in a few days, when we departed for London. It was a confusing journey and I was pleased we checked it out in advance. We had a Parisienne breakfast with a *tartine*, croissant, sugary orange juice and awful coffee in a traditional café, across the road from the station. It enjoyed a fabulous vantage point for watching the ever-changing street activity.

Next stop on the agenda for the day was a visit to Raspail and Montparnasse, so we could spend some time following in Henry Miller's footsteps. We were also following in my steps as I had lived in the nearby suburb of Pernety twenty years previously, with the only writing undertaken being the far-less-interesting documentation of a billing system.

There was a double-decker bus providing services for the homeless outside the cemetery, which felt bizarre and sad.

I'm sure the writers inside would have approved. We found Jean-Paul Sartre and Simone De Beauvoir's graves fairly quickly. People had strangely left their metro tickets with messages on the grave stone while others had kissed the gravestone wearing brightly coloured lipstick. More than a tad unhygienic in these COVID times and somewhat disrespectful. Then a short walk to Montparnasse and the Rotonde Café which was very familiar to me, and the Tchann book store, which was not. A metro back to Concorde to visit the Musee l'Orangerie. What was most memorable about this visit was the difficulty in finding the entrance to the building. Doubt it could have been more confusing. Then there were two women selling tickets, well one really, not sure what the other one was there for. Delighted that the museum was not too crowded and that it was effectively air-conditioned. Unusual in France. Perfect place to spend a few hours on a tropical day. And there were also a few remarkable paintings to admire.

Stopped into Franprix again on the way home to buy some items for a picnic style lunch on the sofa, followed by a nap. After our snooze, we walked over to the Bois de Vincennes where a few folk were sitting on the grass (in swimming costumes), and on the benches (fully clothed), taking it all in. We stopped at a café on the way back to the apartment for an early evening drink. We were the only customers which kind of killed the ambiance. It was hot sitting in the entrance way and my drink was particularly alcoholic.

TRACY – VISITING VICTOR HUGO'S HOUSE

I wanted to go to Le Marais before we left Paris. My memory of this as a lovely area was spot-on. Place des Vosges, a grassy sanctuary surrounded by elegant arcades still impressed. We were an hour early for the opening of the Victor Hugo Museum. While we waited, we had a cappuccino with a nice froth but a killer bitter after taste. The café was surprisingly called the Victor Hugo Café.

Les – Another writer's house

Time to leave Paris and head for the UK. Our train left in the afternoon, so before setting off for the Gare du Nord we wanted to spend a few more hours exploring the city. We took the metro a few stops to Bastille. The infamous prison itself is long gone, but there is an impressive monument on the site and it's an interesting area to roam around. Still in search of a drinkable cappuccino, we headed for the Place du Vosges and found a small café. It was an agreeable spot, but the beverages were, as usual, not that great. Place du Vosges is where the writer Victor Hugo lived for some time and we were pleased to see that his old residence had been turned into an interesting museum. We went in and soaked ourselves in the writer's ambience.

After our morning exploring, it was time to leave the tiny apartment. We carefully negotiated our way down the narrow stairs with our oversized bags and ventured out into the street. It was around thirty degrees centigrade as we walked to the station. We had too much luggage, of course. It had been my intention, when we left Australia, to travel with hand luggage. But Tracy had insisted on taking her PC as well as a tablet and too many clothes. So, apart from a couple of small bags, we also had a large suitcase to lug up and down stairs and, when they existed, escalators. Somehow, we made it to the Eurostar check-in along with hundreds of other sweltering travellers.

France, Au Revoir

TRACY – AT GARE DU NORD - OFF TO LONDON

We found a long and winding queue to immigration. There was a poster illustrating the 5-step process to move through immigration. Designed to be helpful, but was ultimately confusing. I made it through. Hurrah! Les, however, was rejected at step 2, I think because he was wearing a mask as he approached a scanner. He was led away, out of my sight to another processing centre. I sat in a prominent place on the *other side*. I had thoughts about him being arrested for making a sarcastic comment about the impact of Brexit. We were however, eventually reunited.

We had plenty of time to wait; the thing I hate most about travelling. They didn't open the gates to allow us to board until 20 minutes beforehand. All travellers penned into a departure lounge, for security purposes I would assume, were anxious. There'd been a last-minute change to our seats so that while Les had taken care to ensure that we sat forwards on the train, we were now sitting backwards.

Luckily, the train had spare seats so we could change direction. Arrived into St Pancras on time with a quick change onto the Thames Link, arriving into an unseasonably warm, Sutton Common at 7.00pm.

Waiting for the train at St Pancras

PART III

THE UNITED KINGDOM IN THE TIME OF BORIS

Tower Bridge, London

TRACY – SUNNY DAY IN SUTTON

A laid-back evening sharing travel stories over rosé wine on the terrace with our sister-in-law. The following morning, we all off for Sutton Common station for a day of exploring the local area. UK Rail cancelled the train we were aiming for, with the noticeboard informing us it would be some time until the next one: if we believed them! We'd just swiped our Oyster cards to pay for the trip before we saw the cancellation notice. We climbed the stairs to the main road and caught a bus that was fortuitously arriving, and heading in the direction of Epsom. Fifteen minutes later, Les was hungry and twitchy, at the time it was taking to travel the short distance to Epsom, so we dismounted in Cheam and had a rather reasonable cappuccino and fried eggs breakfast at Piggies. The café provided a good viewing point across the high street to a small apartment where I'd rented a room above a sports store from a smooth-talking, French, vacuum cleaner salesman, twenty years previously. I'd resisted his efforts to sell me a vacuum cleaner, and his Gallic charm.

LES – JUST ONE BEATLE

At my sister-in-law's place south of London, we dined in the garden enjoying a balmy evening. After sweltering throughout the night, the temperature had dropped the following morning and was much more agreeable. I set off alone into the big city to attend a talk being given by some journalists and other luminaries to celebrate Paul McCartney's 80th birthday. It was taking place in Holland Park, which is situated close to where I lived for a while in a shared house in the borough of West Kensington. Another street of early sorrows. I shared a flat with five other guys. Six of us with one bathroom, which if I remember correctly, no-one ever cleaned.

Being early for the talk, I had a beer in the pub next door to the flat where I had lived. I remembered that in both the squalid flat and the spit and sawdust pub, I had spent most of my time pining after an old girlfriend, who had moved into one of the other flats in the building.

. . .

The McCartney event wasn't that great. I'm sure I wasn't the only one there who secretly hoped McCartney himself might show up. After all he owns a house in St John's Wood, not that far away. It was unlikely as he was appearing at a concert in the States on the same day, but... he's Paul McCartney.

I'd heard many of the stories before, and I left after an hour or so to wend my way home.

Transport for London, as it is now known, let me down by cancelling the train I had hoped to catch and I had to complete my journey trundling along for what seemed like hours, once again, in an overcrowded bus. I have a feeling this is where I picked up COVID but I'll never know.

TRACY – TRAIN STRIKES

Les and I had another early morning start to get to Kings Cross for our 8:52 am train to Edinburgh. While there are no official train strikes, we had already twice been unexpectedly impacted by the non-arrival of local trains. I'm trying to keep cool and keep humming *Que Sera Sera – What will be will be* - in my head.

Les – Heading North

We took the train to Edinburgh. This was a first for me as I had never been to Scotland, a fact that often surprised others. My excuse was that from my small town in Kent, any journey north meant a circumnavigation of, or a trip through, London. Heading to mainland Europe however was a simple case of a short journey to the nearest port and a ferry across The Channel.

. . .

Our journey to Edinburgh was delightful, gazing out of the window as the English and then Scottish, countryside whizzed by. Our friend met us at the station and we spent an enjoyable few hours wandering the streets and visiting a few bars while he fascinated us with details of the city's history.

As we walked around, I could feel some kind of ailment developing and wanted to lie down, but we continued with our exploration for some time. I deluded myself that I was just tired, dehydrated or maybe was just contracting a cold. The scourge of COVID was at the back of my mind, but surely not? I had been so careful; worn a mask on public transport and in any other crowded situation, washed my hands like a psychopath, been sure to cough and sneeze into my elbow. All the things one was advised to do, I had done.

Les – COVID days

I felt no better the next day, so I took a COVID RAT test. It was, not surprisingly, as I now felt much worse, positive. I suppose it was bound to happen sooner or later. I spent most of the day in bed, coughing pathetically and hoping my situation would not get worse. I tried not to waste too much time wondering where I had picked it up.

Tracy went into town alone, planning to visit the Scottish Parliament building. As the day progressed, I felt worse and worse. By early evening I had developed a fever and was sure death could not be far away. In an effort to avoid spreading my ailment, I moved out of the bedroom and set up camp on the pull-out sofa in the living room. I watched TV for a couple of hours then tried to settle down for the night. I dozed fitfully, alternately sweating and shivering. Sometime during the long night, I awoke, assuming it was around dawn, but no, when I looked at my watch it was just after 1am. I drifted off again and the next time I awoke, the fever seemed to have broken. I still felt wretched, but the sweating and shivering had subsided.

TRACY – VISITING THE SCOTTISH PARLIAMENT

First thing, I popped out to the nearby mini-market to buy Les provisions to get him through the day, waved goodbye and caught the no 16 bus from Leith to the Scottish Parliament. I had of late become very interested in parliament and parliamentary processes. Annoyed at the calibre of politicians in Australia, I had for seven weeks been a Queensland Senate candidate. It's hard to be discoverable as a potential politician when your potential constituents, don't know who you are and what you stand for. To do this you need a lot of time, money and an energised volunteer support team. On reflection, I should have started my research on what was involved at least a year earlier so I had a solid plan for reaching the 3.6 million folk in Queensland who could put a tick against my name on the metre wide ballot paper. Having put my toe in the political water, so to speak, I was interested in learning more about how democracy worked in Scotland.

Non-sitting day, Scottish Parliament

Parliament House was a stark and rather oddly shaped building. Apparently, the design had polarised opinion in Edinburgh. There was symbolism built into the design of some supports, which totally escaped me as it would anyone who hadn't taken the tour. I enjoyed the instruction provided by our affable guide and observing the small glass rooms where MPs responded to their constituents' emails while the public could look over their shoulder. Perhaps this was done to stop them surfing dubious sites on the internet? I finished the tour in the gift store and was surprised to see a kennel's worth of stuffed corgis for sale. Buying one of these toys was clearly a nod to Queen Elizabeth's love of this breed. Then, like thousands before me, I strolled up the Royal Mile and caught the tourist bus around this majestic city on the hill, hopping-off into several museums and galleries enroute.

Les – Indoors in Edinburgh

Today was the longest day of the year in the Northern hemisphere. I stayed home again while Tracy went to visit the National Museum and Portrait gallery. The irony of this being my first ever trip to Scotland was not lost on me. I mooched around the flat most of the day, drinking coffee and eating fruit toast. At least I did not seem to have lost my appetite, or my sense of taste or smell. My friend's apartment, whilst comfortable enough, did not afford much of an outlook. It was situated on the ground floor with the only view being from a rear window, which looked out onto the car park of another building.

I was concerned that my daily step count was way down. The previous day I had completed a grand total of a mere two hundred steps. So today I made an effort to walk around the flat more and got it up to three hundred. An impressive fifty per cent increase but not exactly my usual figure of in excess of ten thousand. Still, a noble effort. I was well aware that I needed to have recovered enough to travel back to London in a couple of days.

LES – ANOTHER DAY INDOORS IN EDINBURGH

Still with a slight fever and feeling weak, I resorted to watching television for most of the day. I discovered, or rediscovered, the limited delights of UK TV. Some shows were still on that I remembered seeing in my youth and I watched them with a strange fascination. What got me though, was the ubiquitous adverts and commercials. These would appear with no warning and went on and on. Daytime TV advertising costs were obviously not expensive. The goods on offer were walk-in-baths and showers, mobility scooters and all sorts of other paraphernalia for the old and infirmed. It was obvious who the target audience was. To allay my feelings of captivity, I occasionally ventured out of the apartment into the building's reception area, which at least allowed me a view of the adjacent street and the Icelandic Embassy, which for some reason was also situated in this area of the city.

Tracy – Visiting Britannia

While Les has been recovering, I've been exploring the city. It's glorious when the sun shines, but crispy in the shadows. The temperature drops about 8 degrees Celsius if you accidentally walk in the shade, which is hard to avoid. I was circumspect about visiting the nearby Royal Yacht Britannia; What was there of interest to see on a boat? Lots actually. Not just photos of the royal family and where they visited in the remote Isles of Scotland, but insights into life on board for the crew.

Have my fingers crossed Les is COVID-free and feeling fit enough for the return journey to London tomorrow, particularly as we have secured seats on one of the few trains which isn't on strike.

LES – HEADING SOUTH

I stumbled out of bed and tightened up my gut - L Cohen. We had a train booked back to London. I didn't feel like going anywhere and was morally concerned about travelling with COVID coursing through my veins, or wherever COVID courses. But we had little choice. Our tickets were not changeable and, with the transport strikes ongoing, who knew when we might get another train? Lumo, the train company we were travelling with, had assured me that the train we were booked on was operating and so we took an Uber to Edinburgh's Waverley station to find out. Our driver talked non-stop, relating not one, but two, of the most boring, yet detailed, taxi driving stories I had ever heard and we were glad when he finally deposited us at the entrance to the station.

On the train, keen, as always, to do the right thing and not infect my fellow passengers, I found a spare seat towards the rear of the carriage. The seat I moved to had no window and, therefore, no view, probably the reason it was available, but I'd seen the English countryside before. I enjoyed the solitude my seat provided. After an otherwise uneventful journey, unaffected by the ongoing strikes, we arrived back in London.

We burrowed into the underground and sat in the hot tube as it crashed and bashed its way to Morden at the very end of the Northern line. At the underground station, Tracy had an altercation with a ticket machine, which happily swallowed her Scottish £20 note, but did not add the amount to her Oyster card. Then ten minutes or more was wasted while a helpful, but inefficient, Transport for London employee fiddled about with the machine before finally giving Tracy back her money. We then took another interminable bus ride for the last few miles to our accommodation.

I had enjoyed the train journey from Edinburgh, despite the lack of a view, but after our seemingly unending connection across the sprawling suburbs of London, I made a silent pact with myself that I would never take the tube, or a bus, again. For practical reasons, I later tempered this resolution to the tube's Northern Line and any bus that made more than ten stops in five kilometres.

TRACY – BACK IN SUTTON

Les tested weak positive for COVID, but is feeling much better. He will stay indoors today while my sister-in-law and I catch the bus to Kingston for a stroll along the Thames to Hampton Court.

I love watching street life from the top of a double decker London bus as we crawl our way through the suburbs. It's also interesting to watch the eclectic mix of people on board and wonder what their life story is.

We disembark in Kingston just as light showers fall. I've learned to always carry an umbrella in the UK. The rain clears and we stroll along the Thames, occasionally stopping to look at the eclectic collection of house boats either tied to the bank or slowly putting past. A few brave folks are out on paddle-boards. Suspect that it would be rather fresh if they fell in.

. . .

Upon arrival at Hampton Court Palace, we are greeted by a magnificent field of wild flowers. Our joy is enhanced when we learn that we can walk through this buzzing, beautiful explosion of colour and critters, without paying the hefty entrance fee to Hampton Court itself.

Les – Seeking 'Spoons

Still suffering from the lingering, final stages of my ailment, I had a quiet day, venturing out only to sample Sutton's minimal delights and enjoy a cappuccino. After so long searching in France, it was wonderful to be able to stroll into a London suburb and find a plethora of coffee shops, all offering cappuccinos which met my, not overly stringent, requirements. I was careful to wear a mask and sit outside in an attempt to do the right thing.

Feeling much improved and keen to sample the cultural delights of the Greater London area, I only had one goal to achieve today. An English breakfast at Wetherspoons. The owner of this ubiquitous chain of pubs/restaurants is by all accounts an unpleasant and self-serving fellow. A staunch Brexit supporter who has no problem employing European staff, at reduced wages, in his establishments.

I knew there was a 'Spoons in neighbouring Wimbledon and we all set off to find it. Wimbledon is usually a short 10 minutes train trip away. But today many trains were cancelled, including those to Wimbledon. We boarded a bus with the intention of going to Epsom, where another 'Spoons was located. I recalled Epsom not being too far away so agreed to taking the bus, even though, I had recently made a vow to avoid buses. But I hadn't reckoned with this particular bus route. It meandered down every side street, stopping everywhere and, thirty nauseating minutes later, we were still less than halfway to our destination. I'd had enough and insisted we de-bus. There are cafés everywhere and finding an English breakfast surely shouldn't be too difficult in England. We found a little café and I sated my desire.

Tracy – In London

I caught the train into town alone with a notion to visit the National Portrait Gallery. I disembarked at Embankment and walked across the Thames to Southbank which is the location for my author conference next Tuesday and Wednesday. I then meandered up to Charing Cross to discover that the National Portrait Gallery was closed for refurbishment. Still, it was a lovely day so I made my way to Trafalgar Square, down Whitehall and past Downing Street, pausing briefly to wonder if I should attempt to have a word with Boris about the appalling job he was doing as Prime Minister. Near Victoria Station, I noticed billboards for Hamilton, a play I'd been interested in seeing since reading the reviews from the US. Decision made. I was going.

Les – Sutton, my Sutton

A day spent in Sutton while Tracy explored the delights of London alone. I moved among the flotsam, jetsam, lagan and derelict. A girl on the street sang romantic songs of love and loss, accompanied by haunting piano music. I bought a sandwich for lunch and headed home, getting slightly lost. The day passed.

Tracy – That sinking feeling

The next day, I joined others in a long queue to enter the theatre. I was feeling cranky and wishing that I was home on the sofa. As I took my seat and started calculating how long it would be until the show was over, I wondered if I wasn't well. I was underwhelmed by Hamilton, which was surprising as I LOVE the theatre, and emerged from the experience wondering where the nearest chemist was as I was in dire need of a swig of mouthwash. By the time I arrived back in Sutton, my throat had the undeniable scratchiness that is a sure sign of a cold. If only.

A positive COVID test the next morning confirmed what I had been dreading. I would not be able to go to the writers' conference and I would need to change the date for my ticket home, at and additional cost of $850. As we were soon to discover, the COVID insurance we had purchased did not cover the cost of changing your ticket. Our nephew moved out of our sister-in-law's house allowing Les to get a sleep in his bed, uninterrupted by my relentless coughing. I had three truly horrendous days before I crawled out of the abyss.

Les – Back to 'Spoons

Tracy had returned from a trip to the theatre the previous day with the tell-tale signs of an impending bout of COVID. As I had, a week or so previously, she told herself it was just a cold and went to bed. But the following day COVID had taken hold and she felt wretched.

Another day to myself. I stayed in Sutton, losing myself again on what was supposed to be a shortcut into town. I vowed to stick to the main road in future. I eventually achieved my goal from a few days previously, a Wetherspoons in Sutton. Why we had not gone here previously, I have no idea. It was as I expected. Even in the late morning there were a few solitary drinkers well into their second or third pint, along with a few tourists and families. I ordered my food and a cappuccino. The friendly barmaid gave me an empty mug and directed me to the coffee machine. I wasn't expecting much and I wasn't disappointed. The coffee was passable, but the breakfast was dry and not overly appetising. It lay uncomfortably on my stomach for some hours later. But, hey, all that for slightly more than £5.00. Who could complain? Beers, which I did not partake of at that early hour, started at just over £2.00. It was my kind of place, and I knew I would be back.

LES – MEETING FAMOUS PEOPLE IN SUTTON

My daily excursion into Sutton included a trip to the Sound Lounge, a trendy café and music spot. As I sipped my soy cappuccino, I was delighted to find that Darden Smith was playing a gig there the following evening, so I bought a ticket. Darden Smith isn't exactly famous but he is a highly respected musician. Quite why he was visiting Sutton was a mystery. His concert was a surprise as Sutton is not well known as a music hub, in fact, it's not well known for much at all. I also had a great, music-based, conversation with the guy who runs the small record store there. I discovered he was born in Mooloolaba, a town north of Brisbane. We had a good chat about 70s prog bands and Americana. Only later did I realise that he too was a well-known musician who had been in a couple of bands I follow. It was only when the trip was over, after I had returned to Australia, that I realised the guy I had spoken to was none other than Danny George Wilson. The leading light of such bands as Danny and the Champions of the World and Grand Drive. Perhaps not as globally famous as the Beatles, Bruce Springsteen or Elton John, but still, for me, a brush with fame.

Tracy – Day 4 of COVID

Well it's Day 4 for me with COVID. It truly is horrid. My throat is so sore that every attempt at drinking is exceedingly painful. I am expectorating flamboyantly with frequent regularity. Receiving supportive calls from my family in Australia. Lots of sticking out my tongue over Zoom for my sister, who's a nurse. Apparently, it's freezing in Brisbane. Must be less than 15 degrees Celsius.

Les – Darden Smith Day

At the Sound Lounge I nursed my pint and waited expectantly for proceedings to start. I knew that Darden Smith wasn't particularly well known in the UK, which explained why he was playing in Sutton. I'd come across a couple of his albums and enjoyed them, so I was hoping he'd play a few songs I would recognise. The concert was a combination of stories from a recently published book - this explained why he was touring – and a wide variety of songs.

Tracy – Day 5 of COVID

Feeling a little better today although still have a sore throat and difficulty talking. I've been getting vertigo as I'm lying down so much, adding to my misery. I note that the Australian government has just announced that you no longer need to declare that you are COVID free to fly. Our nephew flew back to Hong Kong this morning. He had to show a negative PCR test in the last 48 hours and still has to go into mandatory quarantine on arrival. This is of course, assuming his flight is not re-routed because of a tropical cyclone hovering near his destination.

LES – CATCHING UP WITH OLD FRIENDS

Today I had arranged to meet up with two old friends from my youth. I hadn't originally planned to meet them both on the same day and this full schedule was daunting. But, with careful planning I agreed to meet one of them in Wimbledon in the morning and the other in central London later in the day.

Keith

I've known Keith since I was about 14. We met, if I recall correctly, which is unlikely, through another friend who went to the same school as him.

As a deep-thinking teenager, I remember being impressed by his apparent maturity and knowledge of writers such as Herman Hesse whom I also admired. We shared a similar sense of humour too; Monty Python, Derek and

Clive. The sort of anarchic humour our parents could never understand. We strode along the streets and through the parks of Wimbledon together exchanging stories of our lives in the intervening years.

James

James and I went to the same primary school. I've known him since I was 9 years old. He first impressed me by seeming to have no sense of guilt, shame or embarrassment.

Even at a young age, he would swear brazenly within earshot of his mother. He was a less than attractive fellow, even as a kid, but seemed to succeed with girls by utilising his total lack of shame. Something which always irked shy, sensitive me. I never understood how he seemed to be having more teenage sex than me (not difficult as I remained a virgin until the age of 19). Why did the innocents he bedded not realise that I was the good-looking one with the sense of humour? Probably because they were equally shy and were not likely to make the first move.

My first trip overseas was with James. We drove off in his Austin 1100, crossed the channel and headed for Amsterdam and Antwerp. Perhaps we had a plan to see the world in alphabetical order, I don't know. I think I still owe him £10.00 for petrol.

TRACY - DAY 6 OF COVID

Another day when I could climb a little further out of the abyss. I calculated I should be back to normal in two days' time. I will celebrate my recovery by walking with Les into Sutton tomorrow to have a cup of coffee and cake.

Les – Cappuccino UK

With Tracy still recovering, we took a stroll into town for coffee. I was still pleased to take advantage of the fact that finding a good cappuccino in the UK did not present the same challenge as it did in France. Tracy, of course, had looked on Google for the best spot and was fixated on finding it, so we passed a number of other perfectly suitable establishments. Unsuccessful in our quest, we settled for a new Spanish themed café which had tables in the sun. I entered to place my order but was unable to state my table number, so was smartly told I needed that before I could order. Apparently pointing to where I was planning to sit was not enough. Had I been alone, I would have simply left and gone elsewhere, with more flexible ordering rules. But I was not alone, so this course of action was not allowed.

The Sutton Street music scene was alive and well with a young, Jimi Hendrix style, fellow wailing away to the accompaniment of a screeching guitar. It was entertaining for a short while but soon became annoying and I was glad to leave.

Tracy – Day 7 of COVID

My chest was painful this morning. I'd spent the last hours before dawn coughing. Never ending. I was reminded of how I felt when I had pneumonia when I was younger. My coughing was relentless then, and I had to sleep sitting-up. I've now showered and feel more human. Everything aches and I've likely bruised my rib cage. On a positive note, I have been enjoying listening to a thriller by Michael Robotham and watching the final series of Line of Duty on the BBC.

Les – Still in Sutton

Another day in Sutton. We succeeded in finding the coffee shop Tracy had fixated on the previous day. The coffee was good and the ordering rules fairly relaxed. As we sat in the occasional sunshine, I spotted another café, down a side street and later, perusing the menu, discovered they had a good variety of English breakfasts on offer. We committed to visit the following day.

At lunchtime, as it was a sunny day, we bought sandwiches and took ourselves off to Rosehill Park for an impromptu picnic. The local council had organised an event called Art in the Park so there were children dabbling paint on canvas in the long grass. Just two days before I leave for Brussels.

Tracy – Little by little

Had my first non-cough-or-sore throat interrupted sleep last night. Chest still bruised from days of coughing but feeling more like myself. We will take a stroll for another coffee this morning. Les is doing his last wash before he heads off to Brussels on Tuesday.

LES – INDEPENDENCE DAY

I packed and repacked my bag for my departure the next day. I was aware it was July 4th and the irony of it being Independence Day was not lost on me. I'd enjoyed my time in France and the UK wth Tracy. But, I have to admit, I was looking forward to some time travelling alone. The opportunity to make your own mistakes is always welcome.

As this was my last day in London, Tracy and I planned a day together visiting Greenwich, and other city highlights, by boat

Tracy – Failed attempt to visit Greenwich

We had intended to go to Greenwich by water craft from Embankment, but got on the wrong boat and ended up at Tower Hill where there were hundreds of school children about to board. Les started to get a nervous tick, so we stopped for coffee. I wanted to go to Pret-a-Manger and Les wanted Pauls. He won saying he wanted the French influence of Pauls. Groan. Truly a French experience with awful coffee together with serving staff not knowing what they were doing and I was given a pain au chocolate instead of a croissant. We then gave up the idea of going to Greenwich altogether because the sun was shining and we could see an inviting footpath along the Thames.

We meandered along in the direction Covent Garden stopping to admire Tower Bridge, St Paul's and the Sea Containers Hotel. Our route also took us passed HMS Belfast, a Navy ship which is permanently moored there.

We stumbled upon the Temple area by chance, which we were both unfamiliar with. Beautiful buildings separated by secret passages. We discovered a gorgeous café come co-working space, tucked away in Middle Lane. The coffee tasted like dishwater, but the view across the lawn was superb.

We ambled down to Trafalgar Square and Les took a photo of me at Australia house. From Covent Garden, we caught the tube to Green Park from where we strolled across to Buckingham Palace and down to Victoria station.

Temple area, London

TRACY - TOT ZIENS

Snap of Sutton Common wildflowers

I put a slightly anxious Les on the train to Brussels, departing on the first leg of his journey from Sutton Common. Wonderful to see the grass verges on the platform no longer being mowed and full of gorgeous wildflowers and bees. Returned home to wash clothes so that I have a clean travelling outfit. I know this is a ho-hum detail, but having comfortable and easy to change clothes, in response to the too hot or too cold airline cabin, is important on a long journey.

Then I walked down to Sutton high street to 'launder' my remaining Scottish pounds for the English version at a bank. This was the reason the automatic machine at Morden had originally swallowed and not given me credit for my twenty pounds upon return from Edinburgh.

Returned to watch Djokovic play Sinner at Wimbledon. Fingers crossed Sinner triumphs, as I'm still annoyed at Novak for flaunting the vaccine mandate when he came to Australia in January for the Australian Open.

Les – A seat, a seat, my Kingdom for a seat

Busy, busy, busy at St Pancras while I waited for my train to Brussels. I strolled around the station, more because there was nowhere to sit, than in any genuine attempt to keep my steps up. Eventually I stood in line somewhere and bought a coffee and something to eat and managed to find a seat on a bench on the main concourse. I got into conversation with a young fellow who was off on a rail trip around southern Europe. He told me he hadn't booked any accomodation or made any more detailed plans than meeting a friend somewhere in Spain. I envied him his attitude and his youth and cast my mind back to my first early adventures on the trains of Europe. Back in 1977, I'd stumbled off the Dover – Zeebrugge ferry and boarded a train with a final destination of Moscow. I wasn't going that far though, just heading to Dortmund in Germany, where I would spend a year. I also recalled that, after the year or so in Germany I took a three-week trip by train with my then girlfriend. For reasons that mostly escape me now, we visited Innsbruck and Andorra before returning home to the UK. I'm sure Innsbruck was my idea and I would guess that Andorra was hers. Where we went in between those two destinations, I have no recollection.

Around 11.30 I was able to begin the process of checking in and boarding. Again, as in Paris, this was not as simple as it used to be because of Brexit. Just one of the unnecessary complications to everyone's lives, that ridiculous mistake has caused.

As I took my seat on the train, I was pleased that I had finally succeeded in booking myself a forward-facing seat. Previous attempts to do this, via online seat maps, had been unsuccessful. Part of the issue is that, unlike a plane, trains don't necessarily turn around at the end of a trip. This had been evident when the train we had taken from

Cannes to Paris had arrived and we discovered that carriage A was at the very rear of the train.

I was soon joined by a family of three, who seemed friendly enough on arrival, but gradually annoyed me more and more as the trip went on. The husband, who sat opposite me, seemed, at first, an affable fellow, despite his ridiculous hat. He noisily chewed various raw vegetables, throughout the mercifully short trip. Irritating but forgivable. There was a surly teenage daughter, who spent most of the trip encased in her headphones and hugging her knees, occasionally picking at some fruit. I wanted to tell her to cheer up, although I felt some sympathy, having been dragged along on many trips with my own parents, when I would rather have stayed at home. Not that we ever went anywhere as exotic as Paris. But, by far, the most annoying member of this trio was the mother. Her screeching, querulous voice would have made a saint curse. And boy, did she love to reminisce. Each sentence started with, "Do you remember when we were in...?" This would be followed by a flowery, in-depth description of some *lovely* or *exquisite* spot. Her husband continued chomping on his vegetables and the daughter seldom turned her disconsolate gaze from the window. I was tempted to move seats when the train stopped at Lille and a few places became vacant, but there was only 20 minutes to go, so I stayed put. I didn't want to be rude.

On arrival in Brussels, I bade farewell to the truculent trio and followed the instructions my local friend had provided. I easily found my way to the wonderfully named metro stop, *Herman Gebrug,* despite the confusing station signage. My friend, Yvette, who is Dutch but now lives in Belgium, met me from the local train and a congenial evening of wine and conversation followed. Too much wine, as it transpired, for which I paid the price the following day.

Les – A country of two languages

My plan today was a trip to Bruges, or Brugge, depending on which of the Belgian languages you use. This duo lingual country can be confusing for foreigners as most signs are written in at least two languages, often with English added in for unsuspecting tourists like myself. Announcements on trains can also be, depending on the exact location, in 1, 2 or 3 languages.

My train sped smoothly through the fields of northern Belgium, taking around an hour to arrive at its destination. The town was, as I expected, beautiful and full of tourists. Not surprising as it was the middle of July. I walked its cobbled streets and eventually found myself at the main square, marvelling, along with everyone else, at the magnificent buildings to be found there.

After buying a couple of pastries in a Carrefour Express for a late breakfast, I continued my wanderings and took a few photographs. I walked past the expensive restaurants on the square - €25 for mussels and fries, and chanced upon a friendly-looking coffee-shop down a side street. I ordered in English, having been told that people in this part of the country would speak Flemish or Dutch, of which I have no knowledge. The lady behind the counter seemed friendly and I decided to also have a panini as it was approaching lunchtime.

. . .

I sat down to eat and heard the lady, who had just served me, talking nineteen to the dozen, in French, on the phone. When it came to pay, I wanted to employ my French and told her I had heard that people in this region didn't speak French. She laughed, "most of them just don't want to speak it", she said "but they can". I realised I was in one of those situations that tourists often find themselves, where the locals won't use a certain language with each other, often for political reasons, but will use it with outsiders.

Tracy – Sutton migrant network

Joined my sister-in-law at the Sutton migrant network, where she volunteers her time to provide English lessons. The class was brim-full with Ukrainians. All students were actively involved in the activities and were clearly grateful for the service.

LES - LOOKING FOR A CHARGER

After a good night's sleep, I was keen to find a local electronics store in order to replace the phone charger I had inadvertently left behind in London. I also wanted to treat myself to some clip-on headphones which I would use when the large over ear ones I also possess did not seem appropriate. I own a ridiculous number of headphones, mostly purchased second-hand. Often, back in the days when I had a full-time job, I would sit in interminable meetings, furtively compiling lists of them in order to appear interested in whatever dull subject was being endlessly discussed.

Yvette had some work to do in the morning, so I amused myself alternately reading and stretching, exercising the body and the mind, until she was free. Before looking for the required electronics, we took their lovely, but sometimes demanding dog, Peanuts for a walk in a local park. As we drove out of her street and onto the highway, I realised we were close to Waterloo - the place, not the

ABBA song. I thought it would be a good idea to visit the site of one of England's victories over the French. On arrival we found ourselves in a large windswept field which had been the site of this famous battle. There was a monument there, along with a museum and a pub. It was all fairly underwhelming, not to mention, windy and we soon continued on our way.

We left the battle site and drove to a small shopping centre nearby, where I assumed there would be an abundance of phone and electronic peripherals available. I was wrong. We eventually found a place, more of a phone and tablet repair shop, which sold what I needed and I grudgingly paid €15.00 for something which I knew could be had for far less. But, needs must.

In the evening, to show my appreciation for their hospitality, I offered to take my hosts out to dinner and we visited a local hostelry. After one of the best burgers I have ever had, accompanied by far too many Belgian fries, I tried to pay. This proved not to be a simple process. Despite the establishment being large and busy, it turned out they only accepted cash, a tax dodge of some kind no doubt. I paid cash.

Tracy – My departure day

As revealed at the beginning of this travelogue, I had been reluctant to come to Europe because of the fear of catching COVID. While I eventually acquiesced to visiting France and the United Kingdom, I put my foot down at joining Les visiting old haunts from his youth across Europe, which would be full of memories of previous girlfriends. I also had work that I needed to get home for.

The news was full of tortuously long queues at UK airports and I wondered how early I should arrive to ensure I made it through processing with enough time to get my flight. Emirates, the airline I was flying with, reported they would open for check-in, four hours in advance, so that was when I planned to arrive. I made it through seamlessly enough with three hours to kill airside. The news was full of speculation that Boris Johnson, the current UK Prime Minister, was about to resign, so I spent time avidly watching the large monitors for news updates.

The flight was full and I could hear a chorus of coughs throughout the cabins. I had my fingers crossed that the version of the virus I had just recovered from, would give me protection from the other variants clearly on board. A blissfully uneventful journey back to Brisbane via Dubai, apart from the coughing.

PART IV

CHUGGING THROUGH THE CONTINENT

GERMAN BEER, THAI FOOD

Time to say goodbye to Brussels and Belgium. I found my way to Brussels Zuid station, also, confusingly, known as Brussels Midi, depending on which language you employ. I idly wondered if this was because it was in the south of the Flemish speaking part of the city or country but in the centre, or middle, of the French-speaking part. Being a seeker of knowledge, I considered investigating further but, ultimately, decided against it. As ever, I was far too early for my train but pleased to find that there were plenty of coffee shops available. However, it being Friday and the middle of the summer season they were all packed to the gunnels. I found a quiet place to sit and while away the ninety minutes before my train's departure. Finally, after an unexplained, last-minute platform change, I boarded my Cologne bound train. It was also very busy, but I had pre-booked a seat, which I soon found and relaxed as we sped across the Belgian and then the German countryside.

. . .

Arriving a couple of hours later in Cologne, it surprised me to find that the station was directly adjacent to the famous Koln *Dom* or cathedral. I planned to visit the edifice later, as I just wanted to get to my hotel. I also could not help but notice several small electrical stores, all of which had a variety of chargers and other gadgets available, for far less than I had paid just a few hours before, across the border. In fact, there was a vending machine, selling just what I needed right on the platform. Such is life.

After a few wrong turns attempting to escape the maze of streets surrounding the station, I found the way to my hotel and checked in. I took a shower and explored the limited delights of the room. I also extracted the duvet from its cover so that I wouldn't melt when I went to bed. I do not understand the refusal to provide a sheet, especially in summer. But I had learnt to work around this omission in most hotels I had ever stayed in. Fortunately, because of ongoing COVID restrictions, my room would not be serviced before departure, so at least I would not need to do battle with the duvet and cover again. I was also pleased to note that the bathroom contained a standard toilet and not the uniquely German style one with an inspection panel. Nobody needs that, if you do it's time to see the doctor.

As I contemplated past toilets in my life, I was reminded of the time I had lived in Germany many years previously. Through some connections of my father, I had negotiated a job and a place to stay in a small town near Dortmund. I spoke no German when I arrived and the lodgings my contacts had arranged were with a widowed lady and her teenage son. The lady spoke no English but her son was keen to improve his and I think this was part of the reason for the offer of accommodation. The house where they lived was a large two storey building. The living area was on the ground floor with three bedrooms on the first floor. The toilets - yes plural, more on that later - and bathroom were in the basement. I was younger then and my nocturnal bathroom needs were minimal so this did not concern me greatly.

However, one day, I was sitting, minding my own business, one might say, when I heard the lady of the house thumping down the stairs. She was not fleet of foot. The thumping grew louder and I realised she was planning to make use of toilet number two. I was still halfway through my own evacuation so I couldn't go anywhere. I had no choice but to cover my ears and hold my breath while she did what she had to do. Like everything else Frau N did, she did not do it quietly. Mercifully she finished her business quickly and left the basement. I waited a few moments before timidly opening the door of my cubicle to check she had really gone and then, after washing my hands thoroughly, making my way to my upstairs room to try and expunge the memory of what had occurred. Forty something years later I still don't think I've fully recovered.

Back in the present, I unpacked a few items and went into town to explore. As I was in Germany, it was my intention to dine on some kind of sausage, but I spotted a Thai Imbiss (snack bar), just around the corner from my hotel. At first, I walked passed it and continued down the street in search of sausages, but finding nowhere else particularly inviting, was drawn back to it. I studied the menu and found both of my favourite Thai dishes were on offer, and at very reasonable prices. So, I took a seat and was soon eating a delicious Phad Thai, washed down by an equally delicious German beer. I went there the following night too. Sausages could wait.

THE GERMAN FOR MOSQUITO

I had a troubled night's sleep. This was caused by a combination of factors; three beers, street noise, a muggy room with non-functioning air conditioning and finally, mosquitos. So, after a simple breakfast, I ventured into town to buy mosquito repellent. I knew the German for repellent but not for mosquito. I looked it up and was pleasantly surprised to find the word *Mucken*. Before I left on my quest, I asked reception what the issue was with the air conditioning. This was as much for an opportunity to use my German language skills than in any real hope of rectifying the situation. The friendly fellow at reception showed concern but said they could do nothing before Monday. He did, however, offer to move me to a quieter room where an open window would be less of a issue. Once relocated, I also discovered that not being on the sunny side of the property meant that my new room was wonderfully cool and the lack of air conditioning was no problem anyway.

. . .

I completed my shopping along with a visit to Cologne Cathedral, a massive edifice and one of the few city buildings left standing after WW2. After a quick nap, I chose to once again eat at the Thai Imbiss I had discovered the previous evening. Another delicious meal, this time accompanied by sparkling water and not the beers I had had the night before. The irony of eating Thai food in Germany was not lost on me, but I figured there would be plenty of time for sausages and other plates of meat and potato derived accompaniments, later during my stay. After all, I still had ten days in Hamburg to look forward to.

AN EARLY BATH AND A LATE TRAIN

After a great night's sleep in my new room, I awoke ready to face the day. In fact, I was awoken by someone in an adjoining room even keener than me to get started, who needed a bath at 05.30. I listened to my neighbour's ablutions for a while, then packed and checked out, heading into town for the station, intending to pick up breakfast on the way. The place I had planned to grab something at was closed, but I soon found another bakery and purchased a coffee and some kind of filled bread roll.

On arrival at the station, I was dismayed, and surprised, to find that my train had been delayed by thirty minutes. This was not the Germany I remembered. The delay was blamed on something vaguely called *train preparation*. I imagined the driver needing to cajole his mechanical charge with kind words, so that it would leave its friends behind in the shed and take me to Hamburg. Eventually, the recalcitrant Hamburg ICE (Inter-City Express) pulled in and I clambered on board. For this journey, I had paid an extra €10 to travel in first class. The difference between first and second class is not great, but you get a lot more legroom and, theoretically, no kids, so it was blissfully quiet. On my first toilet visit, I did notice one little tyke. He was spread across two seats, fast asleep, so I didn't call the guard and demand his expulsion. We sped north, covering the distance between Köln and Hamburg in a little over four hours. I luxuriated in my large, single leather seat, admired the view, dozed and listened to music.

On arrival in Hamburg, I was surprised and momentarily confused, to discover that the main station and the city's underground system do not have a direct connection. It's actually quite a walk from Hamburg main station to Hamburg north, which is where the underground or U Bahn leaves from.

Hamburg Hauptbahnhof

TOILET BUDGETS

It occurred to me today that I am spending more on a daily basis using public toilets than I am travelling around the city. This is due to many factors as follows:

1. German rail has an incredible bargain ticket of €9 for a month throughout the summer months. This includes all local trains, buses, underground services and trams.

2. German public conveniences, which are few and far between, charge an average of 60 cents to enter, even those in shopping centres or large stores.

3. My advanced years, combined with my prostate operation, which you can read about in My Brother's Bicycle, mean I require more frequent visits than most people.

. . .

All of this combined, meant a daily outlay of virtually nothing on public transport, but an average of between €5 - €10 a day for comfort stops. If this figure seems high, it's because I have included at least one daily coffee shop/bar visit where, to use the facilities, one must purchase a beverage of some kind. This makes the stop more enjoyable but defeats the purpose of it.

Exactly why Germany, and indeed many other European countries, deny their citizens sufficient public conveniences, is a mystery. Had this been cited as a reason for the UK to leave the EU, I may have agreed with that otherwise retrograde step. The UK, it must be said, provides a plethora of public toilets, all of which, in my experience, are free to use.

Despite the exorbitant cost of toilet stops, I took myself into the city today. After a bit of aimless wandering, I allowed myself to be persuaded to take a city Hop on/Hop off tour. Usually, I eschew any kind of organised tour and I soon regretted taking this one. As the bus wended its way through the streets, I did not feel any compulsion to hop off and frequently wondered why I had hopped on. The only real place of interest was The Rathaus (Town Hall) which we passed just a few minutes after departure and I could have easily walked to from the station. But I stayed on board in case anything else of interest appeared. This turned out to be a mistake and when, forty minutes or so later, we trundled once again past the Rathaus, I disembarked along with many other people. I could have saved myself €18.50 and simply walked or taken a local train to this spectacular building.

The Rathaus (Town Hall)

A DAY TRIP TO LÜBECK.

Lübeck is forty minutes or so by train from Hamburg. I was still coming to terms with the layout of Hamburg's main station. However, today I somehow managed, purely by accident, to exit the U-bahn directly by the entrance to the main station. I was sure it would never happen again, as I proved later that day when I returned. But I'm getting ahead of myself. As always, the station was rammed. The platform was too, but when the train pulled in, I had no problem finding a seat. The journey was uneventful as we sped across the countryside of Northern Germany. On arrival in Lübeck I easily found my way into town and towards the famous tower where I had arranged to meet my friends from Denmark.

We wandered the streets together for a while, exchanging stories of what had happened in our lives since we last met. Eventually we stopped at a café and ordered drinks.

. . .

A Day trip to Lübeck.

I took an instant dislike to our waiter who, when asked what varieties of coffee were on offer, replied sullenly, "it's all on the menu." We ordered our drinks and chatted as best we could, over the screeching laughter of three older local ladies who were already, at this early hour, drinking wine. As we prepared to leave, I generously offered to pay the bill. The waiter seemed to have other ideas and constantly ignored my pleas. The fellow possessed that skill, often found in those from the serving class, of always managing to approach a nearby table, take their order and then march purposefully, head down back to the serving area. All the time, completely ignoring my card-clutching, waving hand. Eventually he deigned to head my way with his little machine and the stress was over.

WITHOUT THE BEATLES

As most people are aware, The Beatles spent some months in Hamburg in the early 60s, honing their skills, in various seedy Hamburg clubs. I took the U-Bahn to the area where they played, and lived, to soak up the atmosphere. After a stroll along the infamous Reeperbahn in the St Pauli district, I walked back into Hamburg centre alongside the harbour. All of these areas left me fairly unimpressed. Of course, I didn't expect the Reeperbahn to be buzzing at 8.00am but the days of the Beatles domination of the area were long gone. There was a strong trade in tours of the harbour but I gave that a miss too. I try to avoid most things that involve water.

I was resting in my room recuperating after an exhausting morning of Beatle hunting, when my Airbnb host shouted "Herr Leslie" up the stairs. I went downstairs to find he had kindly sourced a bike for me after I had mentioned, a day or two earlier, that I enjoyed cycling. The bike was a good size, unlike many bikes I have rented over the years, which are invariably too small, but it had definitely seen better days. It had no gears and, even though Hamburg is fairly flat, it doesn't require much of an incline, at my age, to make cycling a struggle. We chatted for a bit about the bike's history and he left me to enjoy it.

I felt obliged, as he had gone to so much trouble, to at least go for a short ride. I set off towards a park, supposedly only a few kilometres away and according to Google, around a ten-minute ride. But somehow, I got lost. I never found the park. I did however find a number of unexpected inclines. I returned home after over an hour of, mostly unpleasant, cycling. After a much-needed shower, it was all I could do to cook a pizza, rehydrate and sit quietly to recuperate.

VISITING LÜNEBURG

I felt rejuvenated after another good night's sleep. I had a vague plan to visit Lüneburg, a thirty-minute train journey to the south. However, the weather forecast wasn't good and on checking the DB - German Rail, website, I realised trains were only once an hour. So, I adapted and decided on a visit to the old town of Hamburg instead. There was one fatal flaw with this plan in that, as I soon discovered, there isn't much of it left. Like many German cities, most of Hamburg was heavily bombed by the allies during WW2 and pretty much all of the city has been rebuilt. On arrival, I had a quick look around the *Altstadt* but, as expected, there wasn't much to see. I meandered around aimlessly for a while hoping, in vain, that I might come across some lost treasure. I didn't.

Not to be defeated and aware that, even if at first sight, a town or city does not seem to have too much to offer, I found a quiet café and, over coffee, investigated the literary history of Hamburg, intending to visit any interesting places. Disappointingly, although many writers came from the city, there seemed to be none who were particularly well known, at least internationally, or, perhaps more importantly, to me.

After a few more searches, I was pleased to find that Schiller, the German playwright and second only to Goethe as a well-known writer, did have a *Denkmal* or memorial in a nearby park. I finished my coffee and set off for where it was located in Gustav-Mahler Park. The statue of Schiller is next to a busy road and a large museum so hardly conducive to quiet reverie. But the walk through the park was enjoyable and I was glad I had made the effort.

Eventually, I'd had enough excitement for one day and returned home. I took an S bahn train and could have easily connected to my U bahn line at *Jungfernstieg* but, noticed another station delightfully named *Schlump* a bit further down the line where I could also connect. On a whim, I went that way. I had time and surely Schlump would be a fascinating place? As the train wended its way, mostly above ground, the fact that I could have avoided a lot of walking the previous day, when I visited the harbour, was not lost on me. The train followed the harbour pretty much all the way to *Schlump*.

Apart from an amusing name, *Schlump* didn't have much to offer of interest to the discerning visitor, so, after a short walk around the station I took a train home.

. . .

Realising I wasn't fulfilling my full tourist quota of Hamburg history, I investigated taking a Beatles themed tour of the infamous St Pauli district. I'd already had a roam around the area the previous day but not seen much. I assumed this was because it was early morning. I checked a few options on the internet. But it was high season and all tours were booked out. I consoled myself with the fact that, from what I could glean via the numerous websites on the subject, most places where the Fab Four had played or lived, no longer existed. Any tour would consist of looking at plaques saying something like, *The Beatles Played/Lived/Ate A Sausage Here.* I stayed home, played a few old Beatles songs on my phone and had a nap. As I drifted off the lyrics of the song, *I'm Only Sleeping* played in my head:

> *Please, don't wake me*
> *No, don't shake me*
> *Leave me where I am*
> *I'm only sleeping*

That night I dreamt, not directly about the Beatles, but about Bob Dylan, who, for reasons unknown was giving an intimate concert somewhere. So intimate that I seemed to be the only person at the concert. Unusually for Bob, who tends not to talk to his audience much, he told us, that is me, a long story about how he had once met the Beatles. I enjoyed the chat but, as is often the way with dreams, could not remember anything apart from sketchy details when I woke up.

TRYING AGAIN

The weather forecast today was, again, not good but I set off, perhaps too early, to fulfil my plan from the previous day, of visiting Lüneberg, the provincial town forty or so kilometres to the south. My host had told me it had been unaffected by the bombing of WW2 and that there was plenty to see and do there. There were, I realised, two trains an hour but only one was a regional train, the other being an ICE (Intercity Express) which my €9 ticket did not allow me to travel on. I set off early to take the U-Bahn into town but the cloudy weather and rain made me change my mind halfway to the station and I came home again to see how the weather turned out. It soon brightened up and I set off again an hour later. On arrival at Hamburg main station, I was pleased that I finally knew which exit to take to get me to the platforms and avoid a lengthy walk through the crowds. The main station was, as ever, busy and the platform crowded.

. . .

A further feature peculiar, in my experience, to Germany, was that each platform served two trains, depending on which way they were travelling. A train heading in one direction would stop in sections A, B and C and a train heading in the other direction D, E and F. Obviously this did not apply to the ICE trains which tended to consist of ten to fifteen carriages and required the entire platform. So, for local trains, one needed to know, not just the platform, but the section on which to stand, in order to be sure to board the correct train.

Successfully navigating the German split platform system, I boarded my train, arrived in Lüneburg a short while later, and found my way into town. It was indeed very quaint, with several pre-war buildings still standing. But Lüneburg is a small town and after an hour or two on the streets taking photographs, I was ready to get back to Hamburg. I'd checked the train times and one was scheduled at 12.24 but, when I arrived at the station just before midday, the 11.24 was still there, so I climbed on board. It was absolutely packed and I had to stand all the way back to Hamburg.

On the short walk from my local station to my accommodation, I called into the local store to buy a couple of essentials for my evening meal. My purchases amounted to €10 and an odd number of cents. I helpfully gave the checkout lady a €20 note along with a small coin but instead of saying "I have 20 cents" I said "I have 20 Pfennige" - cleverly employing the correct plural for a coinage that hasn't been used in Germany since 2002. The lady, or should I say girl, at the till looked at me strangely and probably wondered how someone as old and decrepit as me, was allowed out unaccompanied.

Abendessen, It's German for dinner

TECHNOLOGY CHALLENGES

I had a few empty beer cans to dispose of and tried to find the nearest place where I could return them. Germany is very keen on the recycling concept and pretty much everything has its place, including cans of all types. Although, judging by the availability and cheapness of beer, I would hazard a guess that a large percentage of them are beer cans. I had spotted some kind of device where this could be done, a day or so previously on a shopping expedition, so I set off on my borrowed bike to find it again.

After a few minutes, I found what I was looking for. A clutch of fully automatic beer can recycling and refund machines at a local supermarket. The technology was simple but effective. Put the can onto the small conveyor belt inside the beer-can sized aperture, make sure the barcode is readable and the machine credits you twenty-five cents and gobbles up your can. You can actually hear it being satisfyingly crushed by some kind of mechanism.

Once you've finished feeding the voracious machine, you receive a credit note for the corresponding amount, in my case the princely sum of €1 for four cans. As I discovered later, this has to be spent at the store where you returned the cans, even if you did not purchase the beer there, which is not exactly convenient but, them's the rules.

Following my success with the recycling machine, I felt emboldened and set off, by train, for the suburb of *Schanzenviertel* - literally *Jumping Quarter*. It was, according to a review I had read, stacked with bars, coffee shops and record stores. It also entailed taking the U-bahn back to the wonderfully named suburb of Schlump, which I had briefly visited a few days before. On arrival at Schlump station, I felt I had made a good decision as there were a number of coffee shops right outside the station along with a woman selling fresh strawberries from a strawberry coloured and shaped stall. Stylish. I made my way across a small park towards the main street and into the suburb itself. But once again, I wandered the streets singularly unimpressed by what I found. Maybe it was too early in the day? But it was 10.30 on a Saturday morning in the midst of summer so I could not imagine things livening up that much. In the evenings perhaps? I passed a couple of coffee shops which looked vaguely interesting. However, in the end, I gave up looking for excitement and went home. I stopped off on the way at my local supermarket, and purchased a delicious apple strudel. I later consumed this, slightly warmed, with three generous spoonfuls of Quark. Delicious.

. . .

Having been lent a bike by my Airbnb host, I felt I should make as much use of it as possible, despite the keen wind and threat of rain. I set off again for the local lake. I had tried to find this earlier in the week but had become hopelessly lost, attempting to read the map on my phone and ride a wobbly bike at the same time.

My host had since generously lent me a phone holder and, with the directions showing clearly, I set off. The ride took me past the shopping centre where I had earlier successfully returned my empty beer cans. I continued through a large park and then along some gravel paths towards the lake. A strong wind was blowing across the water and whipping the sand off a small beach, directly into my face. It was the middle of July and there were plenty of hardy locals about, but I would imagine the locale is less frequented in winter. I admired the view for a full five minutes and then set off in the direction of home. Being a dedicated adventurer, I took a slightly different route. A Grand Tour if ever there was one. Arriving home, I felt fully justified in having a cold beer. After all, I now knew how to get my twenty-five cents back on the can.

WHICH WAY?

Twice today I was asked for directions or information by other travellers. A good test of my knowledge and usage of the language. My success rate was 50%. The first guy who challenged me simply wanted to know if the train we were on was heading for Niendorf and I was happy to confirm that indeed it was. He seemed satisfied with my response and took a seat, armed with the knowledge that he was heading in the right direction. We exchanged glances as I left the train and I felt the warm glow of success wash over me.

The second enquiry I received a few hours later, was not responded to so eloquently. A harassed female, with five kids in tow, asked me if the train we were on went to the zoo. Now, I knew it didn't but, I also knew that, "no, it doesn't," was not the answer she wanted and would not be the end of the conversation. I was aware that getting to the zoo required a change of trains but I didn't know where, so not wanting to reveal my lack of knowledge of the

Hamburg suburban rail system, I chickened out and simply said "I don't know". She sniffed a little and directed her question to another passenger who, fortunately, was happy to take on the mantle of German Railway Temporary Employee of the month and gave the fecund female all the information she could possibly need to take her brood to the zoo. I watched them leave the train at the connecting station and offered a smile to the lady who had so kindly helped out. She smiled back and I took that as another little victory.

My own destination was the warehouse area. Reviews described it in glowing terms but, as with most other places I had visited during my stay in Hamburg, there wasn't anything much to see apart from, not surprisingly, some warehouses. True, many of them had been converted into coffee shops, bars and restaurants but there wasn't much else. I returned home and once again raided my own fridge for another satisfying chunk of apple strudel and quark.

Later in the day, I had some small success in discovering things to do when, realising I was way below the ten thousand steps I needed to walk each day to stay alive, I took a short walk around the local park. Exiting the park, I discovered a local Imbiss (snack bar) and a bakery. It was a Sunday and both were closed. Nothing much opens on Sunday in Germany, but they looked worthy of a visit the next day.

HERNE BAY OF THE NORTH

Still keen to get the best out of my €9 ticket, I planned a day trip to Cuxhaven. The trip was the better part of two hours on a frequently stopping train, but I had nothing else to do. I'm glad I went as Cuxhaven turned out to be a lovely place, very laid back. It reminded me a bit of Herne Bay, my old home town, but I won't hold that against it. In Cuxhaven I sampled a few of the local specialities. One was a fish sandwich and again, more to practise my German, than any real concern as to what I was about to eat, I enquired which was the best of the many options available. I ate my sandwich stoically, but secretly wished there had been a Thai Imbiss nearby.

I enjoyed the train journey as, unlike many other trains I had used, it was not at all crowded. I changed my seat once or twice to experience different views en route. Cuxhaven lies on the North German coast and was used as a base for the German Navy during WW2. It's unusual, for obvious reasons, to see many memorials in Germany to that dark period of history. So, I was surprised to see a *Denkmal*, (memorial) to all the German U boat sailors who lost their lives here.

On my return to Hamburg, I thought it was about time I sampled more local cuisine and investigated the row of restaurants and cafés opposite the station. I strolled around for a while and then returned to the first place I had seen, almost directly opposite the station. Their menu board offered Wiener Schnitzel, not exactly German, but close enough I thought. I took a seat outside in the warm sunshine but was soon forced inside by the clouds of smoke billowing from the mouths and noses of all the people who sat outside. In the crepuscular, but smoke free, interior I selected a table near the bar.

This turned out to be an excellent move as a couple, who were already seated at a nearby table, were still waiting patiently for someone to take their order, when the friendly waitress asked me what I wanted. I felt a little guilty but ordered anyway. The beer I ordered to accompany my meal arrived almost immediately and I could hear my neighbours tut slightly.

HOT, HOTTER, HOTTEST

The heatwave that had been sweeping across southern Europe was forecast to hit Hamburg today. Temperatures of thirty-four degrees centigrade were forecast, with an even hotter thirty-nine for the following day. I planned accordingly and set out early for a bit of shopping, vowing not to go too far. There was a large shopping centre close to where I was staying. I had gone there on the first day but been intimidated by the choice of goods on offer and subsequently, fulfilled most of my undemanding shopping needs at a local supermarket, which I passed on my way from the station. I realised, on this, my last day here, that I could have saved myself a fair amount of money and had far more choice of foods, if I had shopped here, instead of the grubby supermarket I had been patronising near the station.

You may be wondering, why I spent so long in Hamburg when there seemed to be little of interest for me there. I stayed ten days and it's true that often, I didn't do much.

The reason I went there at all was that it was the obvious stopping off point on the way to Copenhagen. When I was planning the trip I harboured ideas of enrolling on a German language course for a week. Accomodation in the city itself would have been expensive for a lengthy stay but I found an attractive sounding place, in the suburbs, on Airbnb. Then, I changed my mind about the language course and decided the time I would spend in a group class, being annoyed by other students, could be better used just exploring the city and its environs.

There was also an element of nostalgia as Tracy and I had once spent a chilly November weekend in Hamburg in the dim and distant past.

ESCAPING THE HEAT

Time to leave Hamburg and head further north to Copenhagen, where, according to the weather forecast it would be, at least slightly, cooler. The heatwave which had been sweeping across Europe, faded as it reached Scandinavia, but even there, as I was to discover, unseasonable temperatures were possible. Knowing the station would be crowded as usual, I was keen not to arrive too early. Sure, there were coffee shops but they were always full and a person can only drink so much coffee in one day. On the other hand, the later in the day I left it, the hotter it was going to be, with Hamburg expecting a hair frizzing, thirty-nine degrees centigrade. I hedged my bets and after bidding a fond farewell to my hosts, set off in the mid-morning heat for the station. I timed it pretty well and arrived on the platform only half an hour or so before the train was due.

The train to Copenhagen was operated by DSB, the Danish rail company. It was packed again but I had a seat booked. However, owing to some technical oversight, on boarding, none of the seat reservations were displayed on the seats, as they usually were on German trains. The small electronic displays all read the Danish equivalent of *Can Be Booked*. This led to all sorts of confusion with people who had no seat reserved, just sitting wherever they liked. Then, a few minutes later, the person or people who had booked the seat or seats, would turn up and discussions and negotiations would take place. Somewhat pointlessly, it wasn't until the train had left the station that the displays changed. Those with nobody booked in them, simply went blank, and the ones with bookings, showed where the booking was to and from. In most cases, this was Hamburg - Copenhagen. A few unfortunate souls spent the entire journey in the vestibule between carriages, close to the toilets and with no seat or any air conditioning.

A few hours into the journey, we crossed the border into Denmark. A slightly surprised border guard, expecting, I suppose, mainly Germans and Danes, inspected my Australian passport to make sure I had not exceeded the ninety days I was allowed to spend in the Schengen States of Europe.

The train guard made an announcement. I could not understand the Danish, although I could tell it was not good news. When he made the same announcement in German, it became clear. Our train, in fact all trains, were going to be delayed for an indeterminate length of time because of some kind of electrical fault on the line. As our train was diesel, I didn't understand why we were affected. After a while, a more positive sounding announcement was made and we were allowed to proceed slowly. As we did so I could see why there had been concerns. At least a kilometre of overhead cables had collapsed and were hanging dangerously loose along the opposite track. Once we had cleared the obstacle and continued on our way, there was another announcement to say that our progress would be slow, as all trains were using only one side of the track.

The delay meant we were travelling in the hottest part of the day. As the train approached Copenhagen, it picked up even more passengers. People standing in the vestibule became desperate and turned to the clever trick of pressing the emergency switch on the doors, separating each carriage, so that they stayed open. This gave the vestibule dwellers some minimal benefit from the ineffective air conditioning, but all it really achieved was making it hotter in the carriages themselves. I thought back to the constant struggle I had had with colleagues when I worked in France, who did not understand how air conditioning functions. They would often open windows, ostensibly "to let the hot air out". There really is no way to explain things to some people.

An hour or so later, we arrived at our destination and the train disgorged its sweating cargo. I stepped onto the platform and took a deep breath of fresh Scandinavian air. I left the station and began walking to my hotel. Needless to say, I got a bit lost. So much had changed in forty years, although the main landmarks were still there. Tivoli and Radhuspladsen seemed no different than they had all those years ago when, on days off, I would visit the pleasure gardens with friends or walk across Radhuspladsen and head down Stroget.

I eventually found my hotel and checked in. The room was small but well-appointed and the hotel provided a large seating area downstairs with comfortable chairs. There was also a garden area, usually full of smokers. It was large enough, and the tables spread out sufficiently, to be able to avoid their second-hand smoke. After a shower, I needed some exercise and went out for an early evening stroll. Knowing that if I turned left from the hotel, I would be heading for the popular tourist area of Nyhavn, I turned right to see what I could discover. By chance, I came across a lovely park, *Kongens Have* (The King's Garden), which seemed the perfect place for some light exercise. As I walked along the neatly laid out paths, I wondered why, when I had lived in the city, I had never been here before. On the opposite edge of the park was a grand old building, *Rosenberg Slot* (Rosenberg Castle) which I planned to visit when I had more time. I never did.

Well aware that Hans Christian Andersen, although not born in Copenhagen, lived there for most of his life, I was not surprised to come across a statue of the great man imposingly situated along one side of the gardens. There were many other statues of various characters from Danish history, although I was unfamiliar with most of them.

That's not Hans Christian Andersen

COPENHAGEN MEMORIES

I'm aware it's a pointless exercise and something which is of little or no interest to anyone else, but I always like to revisit places where I have been before. Especially areas of a city or town where I have lived. Copenhagen was no different, if anything it seemed even more relevant here. I had three places on my agenda; my old apartment on Vesterbrogade, another apartment (in reality no more than a room with shared kitchen and bathroom), on Gammel Kongevej and finally the hotel where I had worked years ago. The hotel had long ago changed its name from Hotel Scandinavia to a Radisson Blu property, but the building was still there. I originally intended to walk to all of these places, even though I knew it would involve a lot of steps. I was keen to keep up my steps but I was aware that walking this entire route would take a lot of time. After some thought, I took the plunge and rented a bike. I had been hesitant to do this as, although I'm a reasonably confident cyclist, I knew that, for many Danes, cycling was a way of life and using the city's bike lanes required a degree of confidence I wasn't sure I possessed.

It all went well. It took me a while to get used to the odd braking system my bike had. There was only one lever which operated the front brake while, to operate the rear one, I had to remember to pedal backwards. But, like driving on one side of the road or the other, I soon acclimatised.

I made my way along Vesterbrogade, passing some places I recognised and many that I didn't. I'd made this pilgrimage a couple of times before on previous visits to Copenhagen for work, and never actually been able to find the building where I had lived. This time was no different. When I lived there back in '80/'81 it was easy to locate even without a street number as the building was located between a sex shop and a bar. But the sex shop had long gone, another victim of changing times and the introduction of the internet, and bars are everywhere in Copenhagen. I passed the supermarket where I used to shop near the intersection of Vesterbrogade and Frederiksberg Alle, where I would stand, freezing in the icy winds of winter, waiting for a bus to take me to work at the hotel. I slowed down but could not locate the building I was looking for. I had some memory of the number 142 but it didn't seem to match anywhere. I eventually gave up and set out for my other old place of residence on Gammel Kongevej. I had even less memory of where this was, even though I had lived there significantly longer. But once again, I failed to locate the building. I gave up on my quest and headed for the hotel. At least I knew where that was and, even though I didn't need it, I was also sure of the street address, 70 Amager Boulevard.

. . .

Google took me along some quiet streets and I passed the lakes where I had once walked and dreamed of greater things, all those years ago. After fifteen minutes or so I crossed the Langbro bridge and freewheeled towards the hotel. There had been a few changes here too. Most noticeably, a new building attached to the hotel, housing a casino. I rode into the car park and took a picture of the staff entrance where I had entered, five days out of seven, back in 1980/81. I didn't linger, there was little point. I had intended to go into the hotel and have a look around, but I didn't want to leave the bike outside and anyway, I knew everything would have changed. I rode back to my hotel via a new bridge. I'd enjoyed the journey into my past, despite it not being too successful. Back in my room, I found Paul William's song 'Waking Up Alone' on Youtube and played it, the line, "*I could get back to the place, but not the time,*" ringing especially true.

After a day spent, attempting and, of course, failing, to relive the past, I was made fully aware that, although I was back in Copenhagen again, it was definitely 2022. This became apparent when I ventured out to buy something to eat and drink. I knew any restaurant was going to be expensive and intended to get some kind of takeaway. Who wants to sit alone in a restaurant? But even the price of that seemed extortionate and beyond my self-imposed budget. I walked to the supermarket to see what was available in the "lonely lunches and dinners for one" section. On the way, I came across a 7/11 advertising a two for one deal on beer, which I was happy to take advantage of. But even at the bargain price of 35 kroner (around $7.00) for two, I was still paying far more than I had in Germany.

. . .

Clutching my brown paper bags of sandwiches and beer, I made for the garden of the hotel. I wondered if I would be bothered by mosquitos, although I hoped the second-hand smoke of other guests might scare them away. But luckily Copenhagen seemed to be mosquito free. I looked up the Danish word anyway, *myg* which appeared deceptively simple to pronounce, but I never had to find out.

OTHER SONGS

I spent most of the next morning once again revisiting old haunts. It's a perverse pleasure I suppose, going back to places where you have experienced great joy, knowing that you won't ever feel the same feelings again. I walked along Stroget and came across Mama Rosa, now a grand and expensive Italian restaurant. Back in my day, there had been a simple small building there housing a pizzeria, but Mama had obviously done well in the last forty years and built a new place next door to the old one. The original building was still there and now housed an American themed restaurant. The song in my head this time was Christopher Cross's Never Be The Same - *No-one will ever touch me that way, the way that you did the very first day.*

I continued along Stroget and soon came across a shop selling Danish wool products. This was somewhere else I remembered from years before and it surprised me it was still there. I recalled that, with winter fast approaching, and my menial job at the hotel paying me more than I had earnt in a long time; I spent the equivalent of £40, about half a week's wages in 1980, on a lovely red and white patterned jumper. I wore it constantly throughout the winter and for many years afterwards.

I exited the shop, still heading towards Radhuspladsen and the main station. On the way I decided it was time for breakfast and I sought out a café which had been recommended. As I sat down to look at the menu, I realised the café was situated opposite an old cinema which had definitely been there in my day and which I had visited on many occasions. After breakfast I continued in the direction of the station. But I wasn't taking a train. There used to be a bar in the station that I frequented when meeting friends or waiting to travel somewhere myself. I had looked for it briefly on arrival, a few days before, without success. I was planning to stop in for a beer, but it had been replaced by more salubrious eateries. I stood for a few minutes looking at the area where it used to be and reminiscing. I continued looking for the side exit of the station, which I knew led on to Istegade and thought for a moment that it also no longer existed. But then found that it had been relocated to accommodate access to the Metro line which now served the city. I walked down the stairs and across the road to Istegade itself. In my day this street had been home to a number of sex shops and other seedy establishments, but most of them had gone. They weren't what I was looking for anyway. I walked along the street knowing that my goal, if it was still there, should be on the right-hand side of the street. After a few minutes I found it. A Pakistani themed restaurant which, from the sign hanging overhead, was established in 1979 and must be the place I used to eat at. It was closed at this early hour and the inside looked different, but I convinced myself this was where I used to enjoy a chicken curry and an Elephant beer in the long distant past.

I walked back to my accommodation, lost in a reverie of days gone by.

MORE OF DENMARK

I checked out of my hotel and walked to the nearest regional station to take a train twenty minutes or so north. I was going to spend a few days with an old Danish friend whom I had first met many years previously, during my stay on a Kibbutz in Israel. On arrival at the station, as there was no option of human assistance, I tackled the ticket vending machine. I was slightly stumped by the variations of Danish/Swedish spelling for my destination. While working out which O to use in the spelling of my destination *Sorgenfri*, pleasingly, it means worry free, I spotted an option for an over 67s ticket, which I happily purchased. After the €9 monthly bargain I had been using in Germany, the difference in cost of transportation in Denmark was noticeable. My perseverance with the vagaries of the Danish (and, as I discovered later, Swedish) languages paid off and I eventually purchased my ticket, pleased to note that it said *pensionist* just above the price. I boarded my train for a twenty-minute journey through Copenhagen's northern suburbs and out to the town where my friends lived.

. . .

Look, Sweden

My Danish friends, took me for a drive around the coast of Sjaelland, the island on which Copenhagen is situated. It's very picturesque with views across the Oresund strait to Sweden. We stopped in a small town for lunch. Being on the coast, fish was a popular choice, but everywhere selling it was busy and I was pleased when we agreed to buck the trend and had burgers from an establishment with fewer customers.

In the evening, over wine, we began to discuss, as old people do, the issue of our health. My friend, who works as a homeopath, gave me some advice on what I could be doing to decrease my cholesterol. She advised me to take a number of pills and potions that would increase my life expectancy. I diligently made a note of them.

Let's get naked

Another quiet day in Virum, the leafy suburb north of Copenhagen where my friends live. We visited a couple of picturesque lakes close to their place and later in the day I gave them some time to themselves and went for a long walk alone around one of the lakes. The weather had cooled considerably but there were still a number of scantily clad locals enjoying the relatively warm weather.

I'd witnessed this phenomenon before, people stripping down to their underwear as soon as the sun shines. Having lived in Australia, where skin cancer is a real threat and sunbathing, or baking as they call it, is frowned upon these days, it seemed odd to see so much naked flesh. It made me think of a time when I worked in London and, when the sun shone, people would take their shirts off and lay on any available patch of grass. Nothing unusual about that you might say. Maybe, but the only grass near the office where I worked was on a roundabout on the A4, one of the main arterial roads into London. I would bet that these impromptu displays of pink flesh caused many a traffic accident.

Danes enjoy the sunshine

PART V

BACK TO THE KINGDOM OF THAILAND

TRAIN TO THE AIRPORT

Time to leave Denmark and Europe for the last stage of my journey, a week in Bangkok, Thailand. I packed and repacked, finally deciding to mail some heavier items home so that I could travel with hand baggage. It's a dream of mine to own houses or property around the world where I could leave everything I needed and never have to check-in a bag again.

I took the train from Skodsborg, the nearest station with a direct link to the airport. The same train continues on, across the Oresund bridge to Malmo in Sweden, so I had to be careful not to fall asleep. The train was packed as usual. I amused myself spotting who was Swedish and who was Danish by eavesdropping on their conversation. It was easy, for me at least, to differentiate the Swedes from the Danes by the language. To the untrained ear, they may sound much the same, but there is actually quite a difference between the languages. Danish sounds as if the speaker has been gargling, indeed is still eating, porridge, while Swedish speakers always seem to be out of breath.

The airport was a madhouse, with badly managed queues and many confused passengers. To pass the time, as the queue I was in shuffled slowly forward, I engaged in conversation with a couple of young English guys who were heading for Australia via Thailand and seemed impressed by my vast knowledge of both countries. One of the youngsters took great delight in mispronouncing Phuket as often as possible (it's poo ket, not fuck it – actually, funny, to some extent, either way I suppose). I eventually reached the head of the queue and was greeted by a smiling blond lady who seemed unruffled by the surrounding mayhem. She calmly asked me the requisite questions regarding baggage and destination, almost enthusiastically checked my passport and COVID vaccination certificate and, still smiling, handed me my boarding pass. She was obviously used to the madness around her, and I was as polite as possible in return. I learnt long ago that one should never be rude to a check-in agent. Their power of baggage direction and seat allocation is second to none.

The airport experience wasn't over yet though. I made my way to departures, by-passing the ubiquitous duty-free shops as best I could, and found passport control. I remembered to get in the non-EU queue and stood, patiently clutching my Australian passport. As a personal stand against the stupidity of Brexit, I had chosen to only use the UK one, to enter the UK. It serves little purpose for me anywhere else. I reached the front of the queue, took off my mask and glasses and looked into the eyes of the slightly intimidating Danish *Paskontrol* employee, who took my passport and began scanning through it. I knew what she was looking for, checking that I had not been in the EU for more than 90 days, but I stood silent. I know my place. She turned the document over once or twice in her large Scandinavian hands and flicked back and forth a page or two. Finally she deigned to look up and speak to me, "do you have another passport?" she asked, in perfect English. "Yes," I replied and handed over my new shiny blue UK passport as well. This was stamp free and I explained, or tried to, that I had only used it to enter the UK, but she wasn't listening to me. She glanced through the second document in a fruitless search for the wayward blue markings. Finally, she muttered in Danish to her colleague - probably something along the lines of, "what kind of porridge did you have for breakfast this morning? Oh, this idiot has a stamp missing." Then she sighed a little and, with a vague air of annoyance, tinged with futility, stamped my passport. I wished her a good day and officially left the EU.

I knew what had happened. Someone, somewhere, in their little, bullet proof glass booth, had forgotten to either stamp me in, or stamp me out, of their country. Studying the uniformly rectangular stamps with their quaint pictures of trains and planes, I tried to work out where this bureaucratic omission had taken place. I soon gave up on this futile exercise and went to find a quiet place to sit and wait for my plane.

· · ·

The flight to Bangkok was uneventful, a bit bumpy and as boring as ever. I always try to be impressed by the marvel and convenience of flying, but ultimately find it something to be endured, not enjoyed. Even when I have been fortunate enough to travel in business class, all I really enjoy is the extra space. After all, I can sit in a comfortable chair, drinking fine wine and eating too much, at home. It wasn't always like this. I wasn't always so cynical. I remember one of my first business trips from Europe to Australia. British Airways had just introduced the flat bed concept, a seat that cleverly extended into a bed. Flying from Europe to Australia effectively consists of two nights on a plane, with a very short day in between. For example, my flight left London at 10pm and arrived in Singapore at 5pm the next day. The connection departed Singapore at 7pm and arrived in Sydney at 5am. I spent most of the trip supine, sitting up only for meals and the occasional bout of movie watching. Luxury indeed.

As always, on my Bangkok bound flight today, I dozed, watched some movies, only one of which I had seen before, listened to some podcasts and made frequent visits to the toilet, simply for something to do.

ARRIVAL IN BANGKOK

Whenever I land in Bangkok, which I have done many times, the plane always seems to be at a gate, as far as possible from passport control, and involves a lengthy walk. I never mind the walk though, some exercise after a long flight is always welcome. After my muscle stretching jaunt through a largely deserted airport, I stood in line again. Entry requirements for Thailand had been recently streamlined, following the COVID crackdown and all went smoothly. I had no baggage to collect and marched purposefully passed all the taxi touts as I made my way down to the airport station. I joined the early morning commuters and made my way into town by train. It felt good to be somewhere familiar and I found my hotel with little effort and a lot of sweating. I'd forgotten how the heat and humidity in Bangkok hits you. I spent the day exploring a few old haunts near where I was staying and trying to remember PINs for my Thai bank accounts.

Bangkok shopping

I did some food shopping today at Villa supermarket. I used to go there all the time when I lived in Bangkok, on the infamous Soi 4. Back then, just a few years previously, it was possible to leave the supermarket on Soi 2 and walk through several passageways, which connected it to Soi 4. There was also the option of going further down the soi and using a little advertised walkthrough behind one of the hotels. But as I discovered when I finally reached the end of Soi 2, none of these options existed any longer. The first had been closed by construction work, on what I assumed, was going to be yet another high-rise block of apartments. The others, I also assumed, had been blocked off by various hotel managers who did not want strangers using their previously useful shortcut.

So, as I stood, obviously looking helpless and pathetic, at the end of the soi, an enterprising motorcycle taxi driver waved enthusiastically in my direction, "Soi 4, Soi 4, 20 Baht", said the driver. I had promised myself, and my wife, that I would not use the motorcycle taxis. These ply the Bangkok streets, weaving through traffic and often, on one-way streets, riding along the pavement to get you to your destination. They do this far more quickly, and far less sweatily, than either a conventional taxi or walking would do. Accidents were common and although serious injury was unlikely, the chance of a broken appendage was not. And I knew that my travel insurance did not cover any activity involving motorbikes. But it was hot, and he was there. I hopped on the back of his Honda, clutching my shopping bag and said, in my best Thai, "Bpai soi 8 khrap" - to soi 8 please. The price doubled, but it was further away, and still only $2.00, which I figured my budget could stretch to. A few minutes later, I arrived at my hotel. Happily, unscathed and only minimally sweaty. Another little victory.

In the afternoon, I ventured out into the heat again. This time to MBK, a large shopping centre at the end of one of the BTS lines, Bangkok's urban transport system. My mission was to buy pen refills. These were far cheaper in Thailand than they were in Australia. Things had changed at MBK too. The main entrance now led into a bizarre, Japanese themed, shop with the unlikely name of Don Don Donkey. I entered, assuming it would be an easy enough thing to walk through the shop and into the main shopping centre. But no, the owner of Don Don had made the executive decision to not only assail shoppers with childish, repetitive music, but also to design their shop with a maze of confusing aisles. These all sold the same, cheap looking, plastic garbage which, judging by the number of people in the store, was very popular with the locals. Unless they too were simply lost and looking for a way out. It was like a duty-free shop, where all most people want to do is escape. The inane music assaulted my senses and made finding the exit into the main shopping centre a challenge. After a few blind turns and dead ends, I eventually gave up and asked one of the shop assistants how to escape from this eighth level of hell. She smiled, I assume, as she was wearing a face mask, and pointed to an exit no more than 10 meters away. Aged dolt that I am, I hadn't seen it through the giant stuffed pandas, plastic angels and other paraphernalia. I never did find the stationary shop I was looking for and returned home empty-handed.

Later that day I met up with an Australian friend, who still lived in Bangkok. We had a few beers and talked about all manner of things including the meaning of some recent dreams; losing your teeth equates to a lack of money and success apparently.

COUNTING MY TEETH

Despite the dentally based dreams of the night before, I had a hugely successful day today. Funny how it always seems to take a day or two in a place, even if you have been there, or lived there before, until you find your feet. Talking of feet, I had a pedicure, got a haircut and found the pen refills I had been searching for. I bought the wrong size but they were so cheap here compared to Australia that, if I can't exchange them, I can just go back and buy the ones I should have bought in the first place.

The rest of the day was spent in quiet contemplation, along with a wonderful massage and a few beers in the evening.

A walk in the park

My friend and I met up again. This time for a healthy walk in the recently extended Benjakati park. Bangkok is, compared to most European cities, bereft of greenspace so this new addition is a definite plus. There was a small park there before, which I often used to visit, but in the last few years it had been greatly expanded and enhanced with a wetland area.

Above the wetland are a series of pathways which provide a perfect place for exercise. We walked for a while in the increasing heat before heading to a supposedly English Pub for a late breakfast. Pretty much the only thing about the pub that was anything like an English pub was the name, *The Red Lion*. But it was a pleasant enough spot to enjoy some eggs and bacon.

Getting their steps up in Benjakati Park

A VISIT TO THE HOSPITAL

I could feel what I thought was a slight sore throat developing yesterday. It didn't seem serious and I assumed it was just my reaction to the heat and general dustiness of Bangkok. I took a COVID test just in case, happy that it was negative. After a lazy afternoon and evening I went to bed and tried to sleep. I was still being affected by jet lag and had trouble getting to sleep much before midnight, much later than my normal 9pm. On one of many nocturnal bathroom visits I looked in the mirror and was shocked to see that the left side of my throat was exhibiting a large lump. I poked at it and went into a mild panic. Obviously, I had advanced throat cancer. Why had I not noticed this before? A quick Google didn't help much; thyroid cancer seemed the most likely option. I went back to bed and had a fitful night, punctuated by more lucid dreams, when I actually managed to drift off at all, about surgery, scalpels and never-ending bandages.

. . .

In the morning, I delayed my departure from the hotel and made my way to the local clinic. The doctor there asked me some general questions about my health and poked about a bit, finally saying, "There's a slight lump, it's probably nothing". She seemed nice but this was hardly reassuring. She suggested visiting the more well-equipped hospital, where I could see an Ear, Nose and Throat specialist and probably, if deemed necessary, have an ultrasound. So, I took a taxi across town to BNH, one of Bangkok's main hospitals and a place where I had been many times before.

At the hospital, a tiny doctor, wearing more protective clothing than an astronaut, poked and prodded my face again. She seemed to have more of a purpose, as she squeezed my cheeks, inserted some kind of metallic instrument into my ears, looked up my nose and tested my gag reflex. Always fun. None of this seemed to reveal much, but, as her nimble fingers moved to other areas, she soon established the root cause of the problem, as she pushed on an especially bulbous part of my neck. She said something indecipherable before declaring more succinctly and, I felt with an air of triumph, "salivary gland, you have infected salivary gland, left side." Oh, how we laughed. My fear of cancer and impending doom quickly faded.

She then described all the things I should do to treat this minor ailment; hot compress, gargle with salt water, drink lemon water, before imparting what I wanted to hear, "I give you antibiotics."

. . .

In the afternoon, after checking out of my hotel, I took a taxi from Bangkok down to my friends Chris and Areeya's guest house, around fifty kilometres from Bangkok. The taxi driver I had booked enjoyed tapping his foot along to the music he was listening to on his headphones as we drove. I'm basing this conclusion on the fact that he constantly accelerated and decelerated, for no apparent reason, during the whole trip. I arrived at my destination feeling slightly nauseous and glad that I was not planning to employ the same driver, obviously affected by St Vitus Dance, for my trip to the airport a couple of days later.

I soon forgot about my unpleasant journey with the foot-tapper and settled in at Hidden Holiday House, the small guesthouse my friends own and manage. It's situated on the banks of a river and one of the most peaceful places I know. After a short bike ride in the still warm, but not so steamy, late afternoon, I had a couple of beers and chatted to Chris for a while. I'll be joining him and some other friends on short bike tour of Laos in January 2023. Chris has been organising such trips for years now. A few years ago, realising he had an eclectic mix of participants, he began separating the itineraries and came up with the concept of Soft Nut and Tough Nut trips. The Soft Nut tours generally involve around forty kilometres of cycling at a leisurely pace with frequent rest and sight-seeing stops. The Tough Nut ones are designed for those who like a challenge with days of up a hundred kilometres in the saddle, frequently off-road. I, of course, only ever join the Soft Nut ones.

Hidden Holiday House

HIDDEN HOLIDAY HOUSE

Chris and I had arranged to go for an early ride in the cool of the morning. It had rained all night but thankfully, by the time we set off around 7am the weather had cleared. Chris knows the area where he lives extremely well and can always recommend a new route to try. Unfortunately, though, he is so much fitter than me, that, even when he tries to slow his pace to mine, it never works and I find myself having to make an effort to keep up. We cycled to a new coffee shop he had discovered, but unfortunately on arrival it was closed. A local farmhand appeared from behind some netting and Chris, who speaks Thai fluently, asked him why the coffee shop was closed. "Business in town," was the answer and I realised that, like a lot of Thai entrepreneurs, the owner of the shop was only running it as a side-line to whatever else he did. I doubt that many of these small establishments make much money, and a lot of people open them as more of a hobby, than any actual attempt to operate a successful business. The same can be said for many bars in Bangkok and elsewhere.

. . .

We pedalled on and were soon at another place which I had been to before. I ordered a green curry with roti, not the sort of thing I would normally have for breakfast. But the curry was too spicy for my sensitive palate and Chris finished most of it. The roti was delicious though, as was the coffee.

We took a slightly different route home and the temperature continued to increase. As was usually the case, I arrived back at HHH dripping in sweat and totally exhausted. I spent the rest of the day lazing around reading, writing and generally taking it easy. I tried to check in online for my flight the following day but, for reasons which were unclear, was unable to. I knew that another few hours of standing in a long, barely moving line, was likely to be my fate for my flight home.

PART VI
COMING HOME

HOMEWARD BOUND

My last day in Thailand and indeed the last day of my trip had arrived. I was due to fly out from Bangkok to the Gold Coast via Singapore. When I booked all the flights, I went for a routing on Scoot, one of the few low-cost carriers which survived the COVID epidemic. I like low-cost carriers. They are as safe as any other airline and who needs meals at weird times and endless supplied entertainment these days? Just take a sandwich or two and download as much entertainment as you think you'll need, or more.

Scoot doesn't fly into Brisbane itself, obviously landing costs there are higher, and instead takes the Queensland bound traveller into Coolangatta, also known as Gold Coast, airport. A hundred or so kilometres south of the metropolis of Brisbane.

I had a last look around the Huay Phlu area on my bike. There's a temple just up the road and I went there for a few minutes of contemplation before the heat built up. Finally, I returned to my accommodation and packed, ready for departure.

I'd booked a taxi to take me the fifty kilometres to the airport. I'd left some small items at the hotel in Bangkok so asked the driver to go via the city so that I could pick them up. The brief detour added around ten kilometres to the trip, but, as I was to discover, it would also add the best part of an hour. We set off making good time and only hit traffic once we approached the city. I've driven, or been driven, into Bangkok many times but, once I approach the sprawling suburbs, I never know where I am. They are all similar, a temple or two, a small park and lots and lots of busy intersections. As we got closer to the city, I began to feel the need to visit a bathroom. Nothing serious, but I had mistakenly had a cup of tea just before departure and, despite two short bathroom visits before I boarded the taxi, knew that I would soon need to find one again. Time and again, I thought I knew where we were, and that it would be only a matter of minutes before we arrived at the hotel, and I could relieve myself. But, time and again, as we finally cleared a junction, which I thought would bring us onto the street where the hotel was, I would realise we were in fact, in some other part of the city. My needs became more urgent and I became more uncomfortable. As I fidgeted in my seat, I realised I finally knew where we were and that, surely, it was only a matter of minutes before my agony would be over.

. . .

We turned onto Sukhumvit, Bangkok's main artery, "just a hundred meters now, turn right and we're there," I said to myself. But right turns were not allowed and we sped passed the intersection. My discomfort increased. Another five hundred meters to the next available U Turn junction. We arrived and the traffic light there seemed to stay red for an eternity. Finally, it changed and we drove the right way along Sukhamvit, "bpai, bpai, bapi - go, go, go," I muttered underneath my mask. We turned left onto Soi 8 only to be met by a medium-sized truck, the driver of which, had chosen this precise moment to complete some kind of complex reversing manoeuvre, blocking our way. My driver waited patiently and time continued its inexorable path, as my diminished bladder continued to exert pressure on whatever a bladder exerts pressure on. The road ahead finally cleared and we continued along the soi. The taxi driver didn't know exactly where the hotel was, even though I did, and maintained his slow progress, checking building numbers as we crawled along. I exhorted him to go faster, knowing the hotel was still six hundred meters away. We finally arrived and I was ready to jump out, while he made a U turn to head to the airport. But he insisted on taking me down the short pathway leading to the hotel entrance, very slowly. I'd appreciated his safe, relaxed driving style throughout the journey, but now, I needed to get out of his vehicle and head straight to my personal nirvana. He finally stopped and I leapt out, entered the hotel, waved fleetingly at the receptionist and was filled with boundless joy as I spotted a toilet just nearby. A moment or two later, I emerged feeling wonderfully relaxed and smilingly picked up the items I had inadvertently, left in the room, during my earlier stay. We continued on our way to the airport, my amiable driver unaware of how close I had come to having an accident of my own in the back of his vehicle.

At the airport, procedures and processes went ahead with minimal delay, only taking around twenty minutes. As I had obeyed instructions and arrived three hours prior to the departure time of my flight, this gave me almost two and a half hours to wait. I found a quiet spot and tried to relax as the time slowly passed. We boarded promptly, but there was some delay before we left the ground. The only thing worse than being delayed at an airport, is being delayed once you are actually on the plane and strapped in your seat. I was a little concerned, as I had to make a tight connection in Singapore.

I connected with minimal stress and took my seat in what was, ostensibly, the quiet zone of the aircraft. Quite a few carriers offer this now. You pay a bit more but, in theory at least, there should be no children in this zone. Also, as its name implies long, loud, boringly moronic (I made that bit up, it's not actually part of any airlines sales pitch, although it certainly should be) conversations are not expected. A couple of my fellow passengers did not heed this edict. One fellow in particular, between throaty coughs, regaled the first few rows of the aircraft with gaudy tales of his time in Thailand. Mercifully, soon after departure he fell asleep. As usual, I dozed, listened to various media on my headphones and waited for the long hours to pass before landing.

BACK HOME

Les – Final reflections

Landing at Coolangatta, Gold Coast Airport was a bit of a step back in time. I'd flown in and out of this airport a few times in the past, usually on domestic flights to Sydney or Melbourne. The airport hadn't changed much in twenty years, and still required a stroll across the tarmac to reach the small arrivals hall. New technology had been installed to scan passports. This was confusing some passengers and the single employee, whose job it was to assist the recently arrived, seemed stressed by his workload.

At Coolangatta Airport

Once again, having no baggage to collect, and successfully negotiating the passport scanner, I strolled through the arrivals duty-free. They try to tempt you at both ends these days. Then out into the small meeting hall. Back home, showered, fed and unpacked, I began planning my next trip. Thailand 2023. I also reflected on the goals I had set myself for the trip I had just completed.

Train journeys through Turkey and Europe along with lengthy stays in Italy, France, The UK, Germany and Scandinavia.

I hadn't made it to Turkey on this trip and none of my stays had been lengthy. But I felt I had done OK on this one. Partly successful.

. . .

Nostalgia. Revisit places already seen. Preferably those with happy memories.

Railway stations, old apartments, pubs, even a restaurant - all ticked off. A resounding success.

Maintain an average of ten thousand steps a day.

No problem here. Whilst I hadn't done ten thousand steps each day, I was happy to see that the daily average number, over the period I was away, came to a little under eleven thousand. Obviously in life, some days are better than others. Success.

Do not catch COVID.

My first time in Scotland and all I really saw was the inside of my friend's apartment, and the Icelandic Embassy. Failed.

But before any further trip reminisces, after an eight-hour flight I needed a week to get over the jet lag.

Tracy – Wrap-up

I enjoyed a thirty-minute stroll on Tugun beach, while waiting for Les' plane to land at Coolangatta. This is probably one of the most beautiful areas in the world to wait for someone, next to an international airport. Time for me to mentally adjust to sharing our apartment and life again after a month apart.

He's in a chipper mood, although his commentary on my driving style on the way back to Brisbane is not appreciated.

For me, our holiday is already slipping into the distant memory as I have returned to the patter of daily life. We have photos and, of course, our diary entries which are now shared in this book to help us to remember our travels in Europe and Asia, during this time of COVID.

It took me a few weeks to shake off my post-COVID cough. It's always easier being home when you are ill, and I give my heart-felt thanks to my sister-in-law for hosting us in London, particularly when I was at my worst.

Over eight weeks, since Les has returned, after many emails and calls late into the day, we finally have had our credit cards reissued and received reimbursements from our French bank. Proof that persistence works.

. . .

As I write this, it's six weeks til I take Les back to the airport. He's off to Thailand again to join a cycling trip. Two trips in fact. One in Laos and the other in Thailand. I hope he doesn't catch COVID, which continues to mutate, or hurt his back before he goes. Or even worse, once he is there. I'm looking forward to his stories from the road, which are likely to be highly embellished.

A FEW WORDS FROM THE AUTHORS

We hope you enjoyed reading Cannes Encore.

We made a two-minute video of the places we visited which you can watch here.

https://www.youtube.com/watch?v=mkegPhH9rpc

Great to learn what you thought if you have the time to pen us a few lines, and, if you feel so inspired, a review online would be appreciated.

You can email Les at ljstanley5464@gmail.com and Tracy at Tracy.Stanleyu21@gmail.com

ABOUT LES STANLEY

I was, as Groucho Marx said, born at an early age, in London (England). My parents moved to the Kent coast when I was seven. I caught up with them a year or so later. My school days were unremarkable. Some were marked but usually very badly. The only subject I had any affinity with was English and this was mainly because my parents both spoke it, often at the same time. My career has taken many turns, dips and troughs, a few false starts and even one or two emergency landings.

However, it seems I was destined for an eventual career in the travel industry. Following a failed attempt to make my fortune as a driving instructor, I joined British Airways as a Sales Agent where I stayed for 4 years before emigrating to Australia after marrying local girl Tracy. Fortunately for me this coincided with the rise of the CRS (Computer Reservations System) which later morphed in to GDS (Global Distribution System). I worked in Australia for a company called Galileo and in Europe and Asia for

Amadeus. Both companies offered similar products and, obviously, both were best when I was an employee. I retired from the corporate treadmill 2 years ago and I'm now officially an author.

My first book is **My Brother's Bicycle**. It describes a journey of contemplation and misadventure as I attempt, mostly unsuccessfully to re-live a bicycle trip I first embarked on as a fresh-faced 20-year-old More than 40 years ago I headed south with a guy I met at Liverpool Street station in London. Enfield to Athens on a tandem. They said it couldn't be done. For the re-run I was better prepared, or so I thought. But as it turned out it didn't really matter.

ABOUT TRACY STANLEY

I loved the adventures of The Secret Seven as a child: a small troupe solving mysteries together, often on their bicycles. Their exploits inspired my career in foreign lands and interest in understanding what makes a great team. I love listening to people with diverse life stories.

My friends say that I am imaginative and tenacious, although my husband would hasten to add 'untidy'. Following a corporate career in human resource management and organisational change working within travel, technology, government, financial services, mining, education and health sectors, I am now a consultant and writer on innovation, change management and employee engagement.

My other books include Soft Nut Bike Tour of Burma: Exploring the less travelled roads of Myanmar (another writing collaboration with Les), Change Stories: Success and failure in changing organisations, Creativity Cycling: Help your team solve complex problems with creative tools (A collaboration with Barbara Wilson) and Engagement Whisperer: A quieter and more collaborative approach to inspiring your team.

I write fiction under the pen name of Jane Ellyson.

SOFT NUT BIKE TOUR OF BURMA

A journey of The Soft Nut Bike Tour of Burma was led by our friend Chris. Boundless resourcefulness and a refusal to accept defeat are just two of his many skills. Snapped chains, grinding gears and punctures are fixed in a flash and if it all gets too much for our less than youthful bodies, he'll conjure up a truck or train to get us to the next outpost of civilisation.

This book describes a ten-day tour of the less travelled area of Southern Myanmar. It's called the Soft Nut Tour because there was also a Tough Nut one which required a level of fitness and fortitude which we no longer possessed - if we ever did.

MY BROTHER'S BICYCLE

A journey of contemplation and misadventure as I attempt, mostly unsuccessfully, to re-live a bicycle trip I first embarked on as a fresh-faced 20 year old.

. . .

More than 40 years ago I headed south with a guy I met at Liverpool Street station in London.

Enfield to Athens on a tandem. They said it couldn't be done.

For the re-run I was better prepared, or so I thought. But as it turned out it didn't really matter.

My Brother's Bicycle is a story of (limited) endurance, survival (over boredom) and indomitable human spirit.

OUR SOCIAL MEDIA HANGOUTS

Les
   www.lesstanley.com
   https://www.linkedin.com/in/les-stanley-3969731/
   https://twitter.com/ljstanley54
   https://www.facebook.com/Engagewhisperer/
   Email: ljstanley5464@gmail.com

Tracy
   www.tjstanley.com
   https://twitter.com/tjstanley64
   https://www.linkedin.com/in/tracystanley1/
   https://www.instagram.com/tjstanley64/?hl=en
   Email: Tracy.Stanleyu21@gmail.com

   https://www.youtube.com/channel/UC98owLf5k5GWEjWGgus-7vQ/videos

www.ingramcontent.com/pod-product-compliance
Lightning Source LLC
Chambersburg PA
CBHW072335300426
44109CB00042B/1456